Contents

Welcome
Quakers believe… 2
Quakers and peace education 3

Introduction for teachers 4
Using *Conviction* 4
Teachers' notes: approaching the stories 6

Student resources 9
Student resource 1: Emily Hobhouse, hero or traitor? 10
Student resource 2: Albert French, the young and brave soldier 14
Student resource 3: Harry Stanton, the 'absolutist' 20
Student resource 4: Women and families in World War I 24
Student resource 5: Corder Catchpool, pacifist and 'bridge-builder' 28
Student resource 6: Henry Williamson, the nature-loving soldier 32

Key terms and information sheets 36
Key terms 36
Information sheet 1: How did World War I start? 39
Information sheet 2: Is it ever right to fight in a war? 40
Information sheet 3: Conscription and conscientious objection 42

Further activities 44
Violence/war barometer 44
Values mapping 45
Loyalty ranking 46
Women and the British Army: research and discuss 46
Mediation: role-play a conflict situation 46
Remembrance: how should we remember those who have died in past wars,
    and does remembrance glorify war? 47
Peacebuilding and the United Nations 48

Additional resources 49
Resource A: Graffiti from Richmond Castle 49
Resource B: Loyalty ranking 50
Resource C: Big Grey and Little Red 51
Further reading 53

Places to find out more 54

Welcome

Quakers believe...
Quakers believe that love is at the heart of existence, that all human beings are unique and equal, and that there is "that of God in everyone" (*Quaker faith & practice* 1.02)[1]. This leads Quakers to put their faith into action by working locally and globally to change the systems that cause injustice and violent conflict.

In 1660 the Religious Society of Friends (Quakers) declared its commitment to peace. Ever since then it has opposed all wars and has tried to help the victims on all sides, recognising that women and children are often the most vulnerable to war's deadly effects.

In World War I many Quakers resisted the call to arms. Some Quakers volunteered with organisations such as the Friends War Victims Relief Committee (FWVRC) or the Friends Ambulance Unit (FAU), as with Emily Hobhouse, Corder Catchpool and Rachel Wilson (all of whom you meet in *Conviction*). FAU volunteers worked close to the front line – unarmed – in ambulance convoys and medical stations, treating wounded soldiers and civilians. Nearly a quarter of a million sick and wounded soldiers were carried by FAU ambulance convoys.

Others wanted nothing to do with the war – people like Harry Stanton, who also features in this resource. Known as 'absolutists', they risked imprisonment, hard labour or the death sentence. A small but substantial number of young male Quakers enlisted in the army and navy, feeling they had no choice but to serve. They fought alongside men like Albert French and Henry Williamson (see Resources 2 and 6), two non-Quaker soldiers who believed it was right to fight. In 1916 Quakers were among the men and women who secured the 'conscience clause' in British law – the first time the legal right to refuse to fight was recognised.

Today many countries – including Finland and Greece – still do not recognise people's right to refuse to serve in the armed forces, and around the world prisoners of conscience are tortured. In Britain the armed forces recruit child soldiers younger than they did during World War I. Quakers continue to campaign for the right to conscientious objection and take part in nonviolent actions against the arms trade.

Friends War Victims Relief Committee workers set off for France in 1914.

Quakers and peace education

Quakers understand that peace education is essential if people are to be equipped with the knowledge and skills to deal with conflict nonviolently. Quakers have a long history of involvement in peace education through training in such methods as mediation, alternatives to violence and creative responses to conflict. These methods all stem from a restorative – rather than punitive – approach to healing problems in society. Quakers have also worked to ensure that information about alternatives to war – through stories and activism – is made available and accessible.

In a world that too often resorts to war as a primary tool to counter unpopular ideas and practices, Quakers and other faith communities are aware that there are times when it is necessary to speak up and speak out, regardless of the personal cost. It is therefore essential that stories are told and that people are given the opportunity to reflect on the witness[2] of others. Everyone needs to be aware that there are many ways of responding to challenges. Peace education is at the heart of this.

Peace education is part of the vision of a better world. Quakers are engaged in the world as it is and actively pursue social change through a range of programmes at many levels, including at the United Nations. For Quakers, marking the centenary of World War I must include stories of the intense moral questions and challenges it posed for many people. *Conviction* has been created to illustrate a selection of moral paths taken as a result of the war and provides an opportunity to reflect on the steps we need to take to build a world without war.

Conviction was written by Don Rowe, teacher, writer and former Director of Curriculum Resources at the Citizenship Foundation, in collaboration with Isabel Cartwright and Ellis Brooks. It was produced and edited by Quaker Peace & Social Witness (QPSW). QPSW would like to say a huge thank-you to Don, whose deep commitment to citizenship and values-based education continues to inspire educators in the UK and all over the world. We would also like to thank the children and teachers whose ideas and feedback helped to shape this resource.

Conviction inspired another resource, *Conscience* – a primary-level World War I critical thinking project. Both *Conscience* and *Conviction* are available for free download at www.quaker.org.uk/education. For printed copies please email the Quaker Centre at quakercentre@quaker.org.uk or call 020 7663 1030.

---

1. *Quaker faith & practice*. London: The Yearly Meeting of the Religious Society of Friends (Quakers) in Britain, 1995.

2. Witness is the direct and active expression of one's faith. For Quakers, this means living according to their testimonies of peace, equality, simplicity and truth.

Introduction for teachers

Conviction is intended for use in secondary schools. It aims to support reflection on the moral dilemmas faced by men and women in World War I. It uses personal stories and first-hand accounts to help students:

- think about the consequences of warfare and violence

- understand the dilemmas and difficulties faced by those who objected to the war and fighting in it

- reflect on the question of whether it is ever right to use force to achieve a good end

- learn about conscientious objection as a human right and a personal and political way of objecting to war

- consider the importance of peacebuilding to prevent violence from occurring in the first place.

Using *Conviction*

There are six case studies (Student resources) for students to read and think about and develop personal reactions to. These include:

- two accounts of women (some with families) who were opposed to war and responded in different ways

- two soldiers who decided to fight in World War I, believing it to be a good cause

- two conscientious objectors who responded in different ways and had differing experiences as a result.

The materials in *Conviction* must be used with care, as the issues explored can be upsetting. This is especially true for students with personal experience of conflict and violence. Teachers must use their knowledge of their students to weigh up the suitability of materials and/or the need to provide follow-up support and opportunities to talk individually with students. For guidance, teachers may want to refer to *Teaching Controversial Issues*, a Global Citizenship Guide by Oxfam, available at www.oxfam.org.uk (activities and ideas for primary- and secondary-level students). See also *Teaching Controversial Issues*, a guide by Amnesty International, available at www.amnesty.org.uk.

Conviction can be used to supplement existing lesson materials in subjects such as history, religious education or citizenship. The case studies can be used as whole-class resources or as the basis of group work. *Conviction* can help teachers meet the requirements of different curriculums, including the Welsh Baccalaureate, Scotland's Curriculum for Exellence and England's Spiritual, Moral, Social and Cultural (SMSC) development. More fundamentally, it helps learners take a true critical-thinking approach to World War 1.

Conviction allows students to learn about conscientious objection, its personal nature and the way in which people and the authorities reacted to it. Each case study raises different issues for consideration and is accompanied by a set of suggested questions. Teachers may also like to ask students to formulate their own questions about the stories, and encourage questions that develop skills of analysis and evaluation as well as comprehension. See 'Journey to Deeper Questioning!' (opposite) to help students formulate questions (available at www.tes.co.uk/teaching-resource/Journey-to-Deeper-Questioning-6333933).

Each case study is followed by a 'More things to do' section to stimulate students' critical thinking and personal reflection – useful for group and individual independent enquiry tasks. Key terms are explained and three Information sheets are provided: 1) How did World War I start?; 2) Is it ever right to fight in a war?; 3) Conscription and conscientious objection. These can be used to provide further context for teachers or students, or to help facilitate a 'Philosophy for Children'-style enquiry discussion (for more information see www.philosophy4children.co.uk).

A 'Further activities' section encourages active participation and is designed to help students reflect on the problem of dealing with conflict and aggression, at both an individual and wider societal level. These activities encourage students to critically examine notions of loyalty, patriotism and militarism, and to consider how these relate to moral choices today.

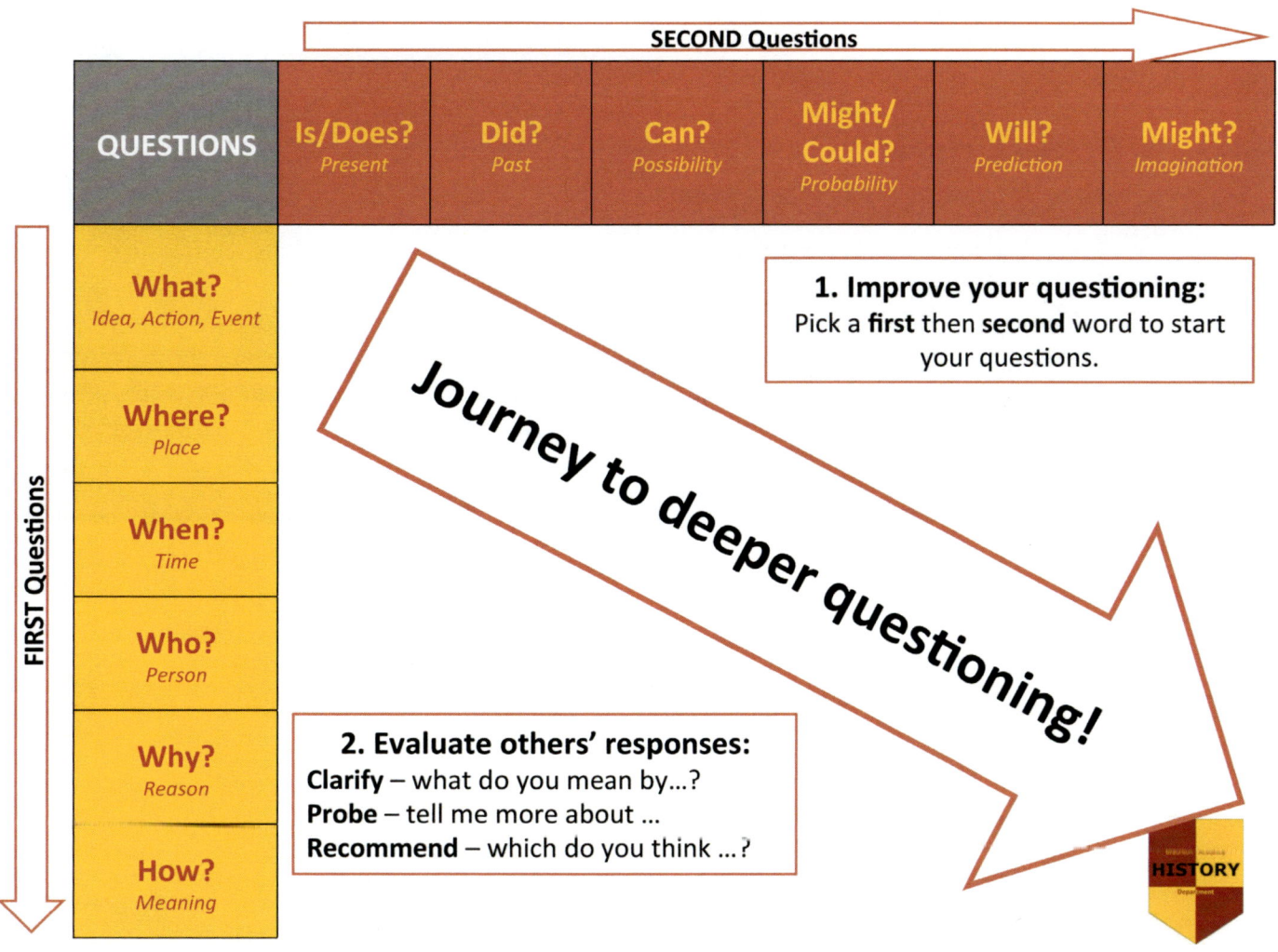

Teachers' notes: approaching the stories

Use a technique such as 'Think-Pair-Share' or 'Silent Conversation' to help your students get the most from the stories. For more techniques and ideas for showing students how history is made every day by ordinary human beings, see Facing History and Ourselves (www.facinghistory.org), an organisation that runs training for teachers in the UK and worldwide.

Facing History and Ourselves

The pedagogical approach of Facing History and Ourselves is based on the following scope and sequence:

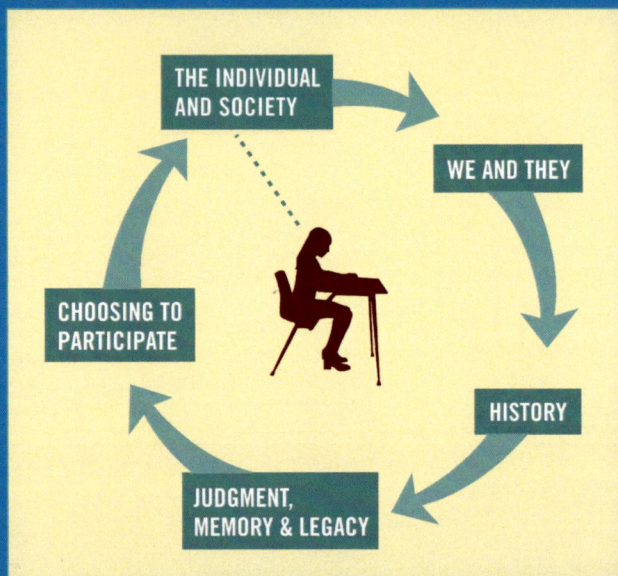

The individual and society – how identities influence behaviour and decision-making.

We and they – students learn that the way a nation defines itself affects the choices it makes, including the choice to exclude those who do not fit a nation's concept of itself.

History – the foremost case study is the holocaust, as well as other instances of intolerance, mass violence and genocide. By focusing on these histories, students grasp the complexities of the past while also connecting it to their lives today.

Judgement, memory and legacy – students explore the meaning of concepts such as guilt, responsibility and judgement, and what those concepts mean in our world today.

Choosing to participate – contemporary stories show how history is made every day by ordinary human beings. Students begin to understand that they too have the power to change the course of history through their own individual actions. They explore what it means to be a citizen in a democracy, to exercise one's rights and responsibilities in the service of a more humane and compassionate world.

To learn more about Facing History and Ourselves and take part in one of their courses, email london@facinghistory.org, or visit www.facinghistory.org/about-us/offices/united-kingdom..

Think-Pair-Share

This discussion technique gives students the opportunity to respond thoughtfully to new material and engage in meaningful dialogue with other students. Asking students to write down and discuss ideas with a partner before sharing with the larger group gives students more time to compose their ideas. This format helps students build confidence, encourages greater participation and often results in more thoughtful discussion.

Procedure

Step 1: Think
Have students read and reflect on one of the stories. Encourage them to underline parts that strike them and to make notes or prepare questions as they read and think about the story. When everyone has finished reading and making notes, you may want to ask the class to spend one minute in silence together, thinking about what they have read and how they feel about it.

Step 2: Pair
Have students pair up and introduce their character, sharing their personal responses. What struck them as particularly interesting or surprising?

Step 3: Share
When the larger group reconvenes, ask pairs to report back on their conversations. Alternatively, you could ask students to share what their partner said. In this way, this strategy focuses on students' skills as careful listeners.

Injured soldiers returning to England on a Friends Ambulance Unit hospital ship in 1917.

Building a 'Silent Conversation'

This discussion strategy uses writing and silence as tools to help students explore a topic in depth. Having a written conversation with peers slows down students' thinking process and gives them an opportunity to focus on the views of others. This strategy also creates a visual record of students' thoughts and questions that can be referred to at a later stage. Using the 'Big Paper' strategy can help to engage students who are less likely to participate in a verbal discussion. After using this strategy several times, students' comfort, confidence and skill with this method increases.

Procedure

Step 1: preparation
In the middle of a flip chart, tape or write the story or an excerpt from it. This will be used to spark the students' discussion. Groups of students can work with different stories in pairs or threes. Make sure that all students have a pen or marker. Some teachers have students use different coloured markers to make it easier to see the back-and-forth flow of a conversation.

Step 2: the importance of silence
Inform the class that this activity will be completed in silence. All communication is done in writing. Students should be told that they will have time to speak in pairs and in the large groups later. Go over all of the instructions at the beginning so that they do not ask questions during the activity.

Step 3: comment on your 'Big Paper'
The groups read the story/excerpt in silence. They then comment on the text and ask questions of each other in writing on the Big Paper. If someone in the group writes a question, another member of the group should address the question by writing on the Big Paper. Students can draw lines connecting a comment to a particular question. Make sure students know that more than one of them can write on the Big Paper at the same time. The teacher can determine the length of this step, but it should last for at least 15 minutes.

Step 4: comment on other Big Papers
Still working in silence, the students leave their partner and walk around reading the other Big Papers. Students bring their marker or pen with them and can write comments or further questions for thought on other Big Papers.

Step 5: return to your own Big Paper
Silence is broken. The pairs rejoin back at their own Big Paper. They should look at any comments written by others. Now they can have a free, verbal conversation about the text, their own comments, what they read on other papers, and comments their fellow students wrote back to them.

Step 6: class discussion
Finally, debrief the process with the large group. The conversation can begin with a simple prompt, such as "What did you learn from doing this activity?" This is the time to delve deeper into the content and use ideas on the Big Papers to bring out the students' thoughts.

For more techniques to nurture and support collaborative and cooperative learning, visit the Kagan website: www.kaganonline.com/catalog/cooperative_learning.php

Student resources

Student resource 1: Emily Hobhouse, hero or traitor?

By the time World War I broke out, Emily Hobhouse was well known by many people in positions of power. A few people admired and supported her, but many hated her because of the way she criticised the men in power at the time. Emily was the daughter of a Cornish clergyman. Her family was liberal in its views and was well connected in society.

At the outbreak of war, Emily's main concern was for the welfare of the women and children caught up in it. In a letter to the *Manchester Guardian* she wrote:

"Few English people have seen war in its nakedness. [...] They know nothing of the poverty, destruction, disease, pain, misery and mortality which follows in its train. [...] I have seen all of this and more."

She became involved in an international women's peace conference in 1915. Incredibly, in 1916, she managed to travel alone to Berlin via neutral countries. Because of her connections and reputation she was able to meet some high-ranking German officials. They took her to visit a camp in Belgium where British civilians were being held. Emily was keen to inspect the conditions in the camp. As a result of this visit she achieved an exchange of civilians who had been caught in the wrong place at the outbreak of war.[3]

How Emily had become so well known is an interesting story in itself, and it explains a lot about how she acted during World War I. Around 1900 Emily had discovered that the British were using 'scorched earth' tactics against the Boers in South Africa.[4] The conflict was over African lands that were rich in gold

and diamonds. One result of burning crops and destroying villages was that many hundreds of people were made homeless. The British rounded up the women, children and elderly and put them in tented camps. Conditions in these 'concentration' camps were very poor. When Emily Hobhouse got to hear of this, she was very moved and felt she had to do something about it.

When enough aid had been collected, Emily sought permission to go out with the supplies. She was appalled at the conditions she found. Up to fifty children were dying every day in the camps. She wrote a detailed report and took it back to England. She handed it to politicians and published it in the press.

---

3. For example, a German woman living in England who had married an English man in peace time and was suddenly declared an 'alien'.
4. Boers were settlers with a Dutch background. A 'scorched earth' policy involves destroying anything that might be

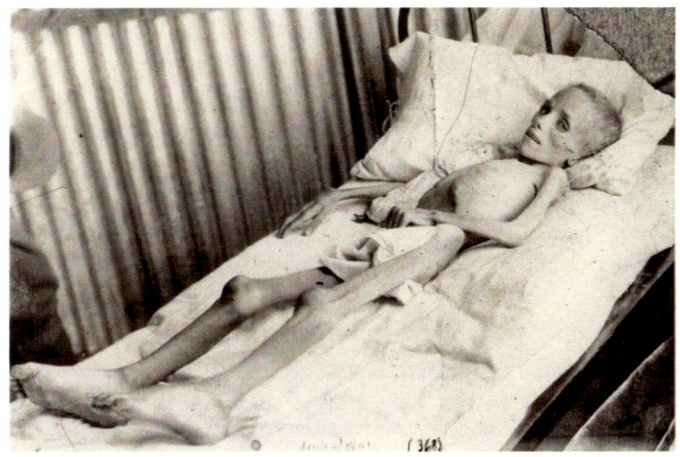

British concentration camp conditions were appalling.

Emily's report told the public about the concentration camps for the first time. Her stand forced the government to change its policy and bring an end to the awful camps, but many people thought she was being unpatriotic.

After the Boer War had been won by the British, Emily went back to South Africa to help the victims of war rebuild their lives and to work for peace and reconciliation. There she met Gandhi[5] and she was very influenced by his belief in nonviolence as a method of bringing about social change.

In the same way, when World War I finally came to an end, Emily again set about tackling the problems faced by women and children. She was particularly worried about those in the badly damaged cities of Vienna (in Austria) and Leipzig (in Germany). Conditions were so bad that people were starving to death. She raised money and support from the newly set up Save the Children's Fund and Quaker War Victims Relief funds. She also got money from many other countries including South Africa, where she was much loved.

In her concern for peace, Emily became a great supporter of a new organisation called the League of Nations, which was set up straight after World War I. It was hoped that it would be able to prevent such a disaster ever happening again.

When she died in 1926, Emily was remembered in South Africa and in Germany for her humanitarian work much more than in Britain, where she had been described as a traitor by many people. But she was acutely aware that war always affects huge numbers of innocent people and had tried to do what she could in those places where human suffering was at its greatest.

An extract from Emily Hobhouse's report on the camps

"I was at the camp to-day, and just in one little corner this is the sort of thing I found – The nurse, underfed and overworked, just sinking on to her bed, hardly able to hold herself up, after coping with some thirty typhoid and other patients, with only the untrained help of two Boer girls [...] Next tent, a six months' baby gasping its life out on its mother's knee. Two or three others drooping sick in that tent. Next, a girl of twenty-one lay dying on a stretcher. The father, a big, gentle Boer, kneeling beside her; while, next tent, his wife was watching a child of six, also dying [...] Already this couple had lost three children..."

---

5. Gandhi led India to independence through nonviolent civil disobedience and he inspired movements for civil rights and freedom across the world. For more on nonviolence see Information sheet 2 (p40), Facing History and Ourselves' lessons on the philosophy of nonviolence, or 'Journey to Justice' at https://journeytojustice.org.uk.

THE CONCENTRATION CAMPS.

MISS HOBHOUSE'S REPORT.

Miss Emily Hobhouse, who went to South Africa last December to visit the Concentration Camps on behalf of the South African Women and Children's Distress Fund, has now sent her report to the Committee, who have forwarded to us an advance proof. In view of "the changing condition of the camps," Miss Hobhouse writes, "it is hardly possible to draw up an ordinary conventional report." Her account of what she has seen is therefore given in the form in which it "was written down day by day"; and in fact consists of portions of a series of letters extending over the three months from January 22 to April 22. To this is appended an important series of recommendations for the reform of the camps, and finally, as a lengthy appendix, a series of statements taken down from the Boer women and children themselves. The following extracts from the letters are representative:—

JANUARY 22.

I had a splendid truck given me at Capetown, through the kind co-operation of Sir Alfred Milner—a large double-covered one, capable of holding 12 tons. I took £200 worth of groceries, besides all the bales of clothing I could muster. The truck left Capetown the day before myself, was hitched on to my train at De Aar, and so arrived when I did. The first thing next day was to go down to the goods station, claim the truck, and arrange for its unloading. This morning I have spent arranging all my stores—unpacking and sorting them. Going through the Karoo it was very hot, and the second day there were horrible dust-storms, varied by thunderstorms. The sand penetrated through closed windows and doors, filled eyes and ears, turned my hair red, and covered everything like a tablecloth. From Colesberg on it was a desolate outlook. The land seemed dead and silent as far as the eye could reach, absolutely without life, only carcases of horses, mules, and cattle, with a sort of acute anguish in their look, and bleached bones and refuse of many kinds. I saw a few burnt farms, but those unburnt seemed still and lifeless also, and no work is going on in the fields. Really, the line the whole way up is a string of Tommies, yawning at their posts, and these always crowded to the carriage windows to beg for newspapers, or anything, they said, to pass the time. I gave them all I had, and all my novels. . . . But I must pass on to tell you about the Women's Camp, which, after all, is the central point of interest.

THE BLOEMFONTEIN CAMP.

JANUARY 26.

The exile camp here is a good two miles from the town, dumped down on the southern slope of a kopje, right out on to the bare brown veld, not a vestige of a tree in any direction, nor shade of any description. It was about four o'clock of a scorching afternoon when I set foot in the camp, and I can't tell you what I felt like, so I won't try.

I began by finding a woman whose sister I had met in Capetown. It is such a puzzle to find your way in a village of bell tents, no streets or names or numbers. There are nearly 2,000* people in this one camp, of which some few are men—they call them "hands up" men—and over 900* children.

Imagine the heat outside the tents and the suffocation inside! We sat on their khaki blankets, rolled up, inside Mrs. B.'s tent; and the sun blazed through the single canvas, and the flies lay thick and black on everything; no chair, no table, nor any room for such; only a deal box, standing on its end, served as a wee pantry. In this tiny tent live Mrs. B.'s five children (three quite grown up) and a little Kaffir servant girl. Many tents have more occupants. Mrs. P. came in, and Mrs. R. and others, and they told me their stories, and we cried together, and even laughed together, and chatted bad Dutch and bad English all the afternoon. On wet nights the water streams down through the canvas and comes flowing in, as it knows how to do in this country, under the flap of the tent, and wets their blankets as they lie on the ground. While we sat there a snake came in. They said it was a puff adder, very poisonous, so they all ran out, and I attacked the creature with my parasol. I could not bear to think the thing should be at large in a community mostly sleeping on the ground. After a struggle I wounded it, and then a man came with a mallet and finished it off.

Manchester Guardian archive, 19 June 1901:
The South African concentration camps. Emily Hobhouse reports from inside the internment centres where Boer women and children face squalor and starvation. The paper's stance on the Boer War, and its willingness to publish unpalatable truths, was deeply unpopular to many in Britain and led to threats against *Guardian* workers.

Resource 1a:
things to think and talk about

1. Which passages in the portrait of Emily Hobhouse tell us something about the kind of person she was? Underline these parts of the text.
2. How might Emily have defended herself against the charge of being a traitor to her country for criticising the British 'concentration' camps?
3. In your opinion, was Emily right to focus her attention on the needs of people in Germany and Austria after the war? Why do you think she did this?
4. Emily is a national heroine in South Africa to this day. Do you think she ought to be better known in Britain? To what extent do you think her actions could be seen as a good example for others to follow?
5. Emily's work focused on relief efforts but also on peacebuilding. What forms did this take? In your opinion, how important is peacebuilding and why?

More things to do

Can you find out more about women who have taken a stand for peace:

- Find out about the Women's International League for Peace and Freedom (WILPF) and the International Women's Congress against World War I that took place in The Hague, the Netherlands, in 1915. See www.wilpfinternational.org and watch 'These Dangerous Women", a documentary about women who tried to stop World War 1.

- What was the purpose of founding WILPF? What campaigns is WILPF involved with today?

- Discover more women peace heroes: The Nobel Peace Prize has been awarded annually since 1901, but only 12 women have received it. In 2005 1,000 women peacebuilders from 150 countries were nominated as part of the 1,000 Women for the Nobel Peace Prize 2005 Project. Although the project did not receive the Nobel Peace Prize that year, it succeeded in creating a campaign to help make women's peacebuilding efforts around the world more recognised and supported. Discover these inspiring women Peace Heroes at: www.doonething.org/heroes/1000peacewomen

- Watch the inspirational film *Pray the devil back to hell* about the courageous Liberian women – ordinary mothers, grandmothers, aunts and daughters – who used active nonviolence to end the bloody civil war and bring peace to their shattered country: www.praythedevilbacktohell.com

Student resource 2: Albert French, the young and brave soldier

Albert French was only 15 when World War I broke out. By this time he had left school and got a job at the local railway works in Wolverton[6] as an apprentice engineer. He was tall, dark-haired and looked older than he really was. Albert's mother had died when he was young and he and his two brothers were looked after by his older sister May. We do not know much about what Albert knew or thought about the war at this stage, but we do know that he belonged to the Church Lads' Brigade, which is rather like the Scouts.

A year later, in 1915, we know that Albert left his job at the railway works and, without telling his father, went off to join the army. He enlisted with the King's Royal Rifles, which was based in London. His father tried to stop him, but it was too late. Albert had lied to the army about his age (he said he was 19).

Albert's first letters home suggest that being in the army was exciting, and he was looking forward to doing well and getting promoted:

> 6 November 1915
>
> "I am going to try to be a lance-corporal before Christmas. Last Friday we were short of section commanders, so the commander asked me to command one section. I had to drill them, and the commander said I was very good. He said I was getting on quick. So, you see I am getting on all right, and stand a good chance of rising from the ranks. [...] I'm going to [...] buy a military book of some kind every week, and become a Major-General some day."

Albert then went on to say that one evening he and some friends had gone to the "Salvation Army Headquarters" and had been "converted". He wrote:

> "It is a bigger thing than being confirmed. You have your sins forgiven and promise God not to swear, steal, lie, deceive, misconduct yourself, and to obey the 10 commandments. [...] There are some soldiers who have an opinion that this war will be the end of the world, but whether it is or whether it is not, I have made a start for the good. I hope you do not think I am barmy."

6. Wolverton is now part of Milton Keynes in Buckinghamshire.

The training partly involved toughening up the soldiers and preparing them for what would lie ahead when they got to the front line:

> "We have had a lot of snow here, and it's fearfully cold at present here. The other day in a big field we had to lay on a large plain quite still, half an hour, and there was a terrible cold cutting wind all the while. Some of the chaps were absolutely groaning with the cold. I have just about got used to the cold, but I had to exert all my powers to stand that."

In others letters Albert describes taking part in mock battles, night marches and the like. He was hoping to go home at Christmas but it wasn't until January that he managed to see his family. On 23 January, once he was back at base, he wrote:

> "I enjoyed my week's furlough [leave] especially with Violet on Saturday and Sunday. It was nice being at home, and it was rotten having to come back here, it's such a dreary, out of the way place. [...] But now I'm in the army, I'm going to stick. It's not such an easy job as you at first think, but now I'm going to stick, whatever happens, for the duration of the war, at any rate, and for a good while after if I feel like it. I'm out to make a man of myself. [...] I might as well tell you that I rather took a liking to Violet while I was home and I hope she writes to me."

Some while later Albert's training was coming to a close and he wrote:

> "We finished our musketry course this morning [training in shooting]. In the 1st two parts I did splendid, but in the 3rd and final part, I did not do so well. The 2 first parts do not really count, so I have truly turned out a 2nd class shot. [...] We had to do one practice in our gas helmets today. We had to put them on, and fire five rounds rapid in a minute. We had to run with them on too. Some of the fellows were spluttering and gasping for breath. [...] They are very simply made, most of them out of old shirts. They stink and smell of chemicals."

Shortly after this, Albert was writing from France:

"The sergeant's just gave me one of your letters, and by the date it's taken three days to come. [...] I had a letter from Violet Cox two or three days ago. I've had about a dozen letters from Violet all together, and you can guess I've sent her about 13. [...] I shan't stop in the army after the war, it's not good enough. We don't get as much [food] as we did at Aldershot. If you don't keep your eyes skinned, you don't get any at all. [...] We shall be popping away at the Germans pretty shortly, and as long as I don't get popped it will be alright, I guess."

Albert and his fellow soldiers were sent to the front near Ploegsteert in Belgium (or Plug Street, as the British soldiers called it). This was where Henry Williamson (who you meet in Resource 6) had been nearly two years earlier. The front had hardly moved in all that time. On 4 June 1916 he wrote again to his sister May:

"We are quartered in 'Musty Villa' which is the name given to our dug out. We have to do our grub up securely, or half of it disappears to the rats and mice. [...] The shells do not make so much row as I thought they would. They make a whirling tearing noise and scream slightly. You can hear them rush through the air, but you can't see them going. They make a big hole and plenty of smoke when they burst, and bits fly about 50 yards. The bullets make a long drawn out pinging noise. Well dear May, must now come to a close with the best of my love to you.

Your loving brother,

Albert
XXXXXXXX
XXXXXXXX"

The next letter Albert's family received from the front came not from him but from an officer. It was addressed to Albert's father:

> "Sir,
>
> I regret to have to report the death of your son C7259 Rfn. [Rifleman] A. French, who was killed by machine gun fire, whilst with a working party June 15th 1916. He was a very good soldier, although so young, and a willing worker, who made many friends in the company. He is sadly missed."

And on the same day, the company chaplain also wrote to Mr French:

> 17 June 1916
>
> "Dear Mr. French,
>
> I am very sorry to have to write to you and inform you that your dear son was killed in action on June 15th. He died as every true soldier wishes to die - doing his duty nobly for King and Country. He was doing some sand-bagging on the parapet of the trench when four bullets from a machine gun hit him and he died instantaneously.
>
> He lies buried amid brave comrades in a wood, and his grave is carefully tended by his friends in his battalion...
>
> Yours sincerely
>
> M.A.O. Mayne
>
> C of E Chaplain"

Note
At first there was no reference to Albert's very young age on his headstone. As a result of a successful campaign this was added, and now his grave is one of those most often visited by students touring the battlefields of the Western Front.

The story of Albert French and the full collection of his letters can be found on the Milton Keynes Heritage Association website at www.mkheritage.co.uk/la.

Resource 2a:
things to think and talk about

1. Which passages in the portrait of Albert French tell us something about the kind of person he was? Underline these parts of the text. Why do you think he joined the army?
2. Albert was one of the youngest soldiers to fight in World War I. Do you think someone so young could really appreciate what he was signing up for? Is there any evidence to suggest that Albert did not fully realise what war was like?
3. In World War I the youngest that recruits could join up was officially 18, and only those older than 19 were supposed to be sent to fight. As in Albert's case, many boys were actually much younger. What age limits would you set for enlistment today?
4. It was not uncommon in World War I for young men to enlist as a way of seeking adventure. Does this happen today? What might you say to someone taking this attitude to help them make an informed choice?
5. Why do you think students so often go to Albert's grave when visiting the Western Front?

More things to do
Ask your students to:

- Research and debate arguments for and against raising the UK age of military recruitment to 18

- Debate the role of the military in education.

Should the military recruitment age be raised to 18? Today Britain is the only country in the EU to recruit under-18s into the armed forces. The Ministry of Defence (MoD) currently enlists soldiers at 16 (with parental consent), but only deploys them to fight from 18. This has been criticised by the UN Committee on the Rights of the Child. Quakers in Britain joined Child Soldiers International and a group of churches and children's organisations to call for the MoD to stop recruiting under-18s. In an open letter to the Minister of State for the Armed Forces they said: "Current recruitment policy channels the youngest, most disadvantaged recruits into the most dangerous frontline combat roles. According to *The Scotsman*, those recruited at 16 have faced double the risk of fatality of adult recruits in Afghanistan". Child Soldiers International is campaigning to raise the recruitment age to 18 in the UK. Britain is one of just 20 countries to still allow their armed forces to recruit young people at 16. Organisations like ForcesWatch and Medact have written about the greater problems faced by these younger recruits. See www.child-soldiers.org/dontenlistat16.

What role should the military play in British schools? The armed forces visit thousands of UK schools each year, offering presentations, resources and military-led activities. When he was Secretary of State for Education, Michael Gove believed that "every child can benefit from the values of a military ethos". The Department for Education is integrating military-led activities into Britain's education system. But organisations like ForcesWatch, Quakers in Britain and Veterans for Peace UK continue to work to challenge military involvement in schools.

Quaker Peace & Social Witness has created a poster to highlight the increasing presence of the military in society. Download at www.quaker.org.uk/resources/free-resources/teaching-resources-2

Go to www.unseenmarch.org.uk to view a five-minute film on militarism in education. Also look out for the new documentary *War School*, from POW Productions.

Today Britain is the only country in the EU to recruit under-18s into the armed forces.
Photo © UK MoD Crown Copyright 2011

Student resource 3: Harry Stanton, the 'absolutist'

Harry Stanton lived in Luton. His father was a blacksmith. When the war broke out Harry took the Quaker view that war is wrong. He was well aware that most people thought differently, but the comments of people in the street and in the papers just made him stronger. He wrote:

"Now and again, as I met men and women whose convictions were leading them along the same unpopular course, came the feeling that here was something worth doing…"

Harry tried to persuade his friends not to enlist. Many of them agreed with him that war was evil but that, on balance, England was right to resist the Germans. Harry realised that people like him had to support each other at this difficult time. So he joined the No-Conscription[7] Fellowship (NCF). Members of the NCF were against conscription because they thought human life was sacred. And the socialists among them believed they had no quarrel with the German working classes. The NCF opposed the campaign to bring in conscription in 1916. It also fought for a law allowing people to opt out of fighting on grounds of conscience, known as the 'conscience clause'.

By 1916 the war was not going well. Hundreds of thousands of young men had been killed and more were urgently needed. So conscription was introduced for men between the ages of 18 and 41, if they were fit enough. Those who refused to fight were taken before a tribunal and required to prove that they were not simply trying to dodge the call-up. If the men were not believed they were taken off to join the army straight away. If they were believed, they were offered the chance to work for the war in a way that avoided fighting. One option was to join a medical corps; working on the land was another. If they refused these alternatives to fighting, they would be sent to prison. Men who refused to fight because of their beliefs were called 'conscientious objectors' (or COs).

Some officers treated COs with respect, but most of them thought they were traitors and cowards. All kinds of methods were tried to break their spirits. For example, they were often verbally abused, beaten, put in cold, dark cells, hosed down with cold water, kept in isolation and forbidden to speak to other prisoners. In May 1916 another tactic was tried. Around fifty COs were taken from prison and sent to the front line in France, where anyone refusing to fight could be shot. Harry Stanton was among them. He and two or three others were taken to a special punishment unit for 28 days. Harry described what happened next. Someone had made a wooden framework consisting of…

"…uprights 4 or 5 yards apart with connecting beams at a height of about 5 feet. We were placed with our backs to the posts, and arms outstretched. Our ankles were then tied together and our arms tied tightly at the wrists to the cross beams. We were to remain in this position for two hours. For those of us who were of average height the strain upon our arms was just bearable, though our wrists quickly became numbed, but for those who

Dyce Prison Camp near Aberdeen, Scotland, 1916.

7. Conscription is the compulsory call-up into the armed forces.

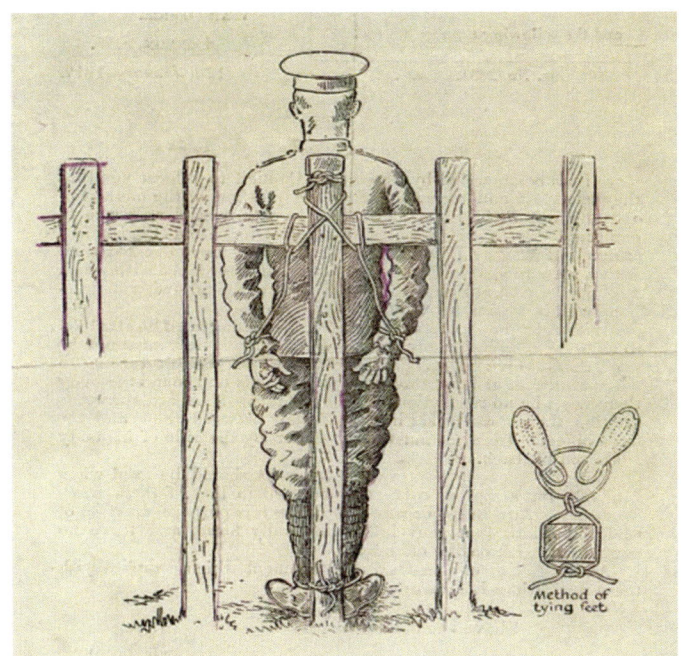

Field Punishment No. 1 replaced flogging in the British Army. It was used for those who disobeyed orders on active service.

were shorter, the punishment was painful in the extreme."

After Harry and someone else had attempted to stand on some boards to stay out of the mud beneath their feet, they were punished even more severely. This time they were tied to a double barbed-wire fence:

"We two were… placed with our faces to the wire of the inner fence and tied in the usual manner at the wrists and ankles. …and I found myself drawn so closely into the fence that when I wished to turn my head I had to do so very slowly and cautiously to avoid my face being torn by the barbs. To make matters worse it came on to rain, and a cold wind blew straight across the top of the hill."

However, the resistance of Harry and the others held up. Next, they were marched off under armed guard to Boulogne. A soldier told Harry that they were being taken to the front line "so that you can be shot if you still disobey orders". Another soldier added that he would rather shoot the officer giving the order than shoot these resisters. "I came out here to fight the Germans, not to murder Englishmen", he said.

Things came to a head when the men were finally charged and found guilty of a range of military crimes. The officer read out the men's crimes and then declared, "The sentence of the court is to suffer death by being shot." Then, after a pause, he added, "Confirmed by the Commander-in-Chief." The men thought that was it, but their sentences were then reduced to ten years' hard labour.

The authorities had stepped back from the idea that any good would come from executing the men.[8] Harry Stanton was sent to Dyce Labour Camp in Scotland, where the men were put to work breaking rocks. These could be used, for example, in road building. Two hundred men were interned there, enduring harsh conditions such as leaky tents, poor sanitation, little to eat, and no treatment for illness.[9] After a while Harry thought that doing this kind of work was wrong because it might allow other men to go and fight. When he refused to break any more rocks he was sent back to prison. Men like Harry who wouldn't cooperate with the authorities in any way, and also refused to do alternative work for the war effort, were called 'absolutists'.

During the war, the treatment given to the COs caused some to die and others to suffer physical and mental illnesses.

Harold Bing recalled: "Some died in prison; some went mad; some broke down in health completely and never really recovered; some were discharged because they were on the point of death; some suffered terribly from insomnia… For many people it was extremely hard."

---

8. This decision may have been influenced by the attention that the NCF were able to bring to the case of the COs in France. The NCF had ensured questions were asked in the House of Commons and two people, the Reverend F.B. Meyer and Hubert Peet (a Quaker journalist who features in Resource 4), managed to get permission to visit the men in France to report on their conditions.
9. A young CO called Walter Roberts died as a result of this treatment.

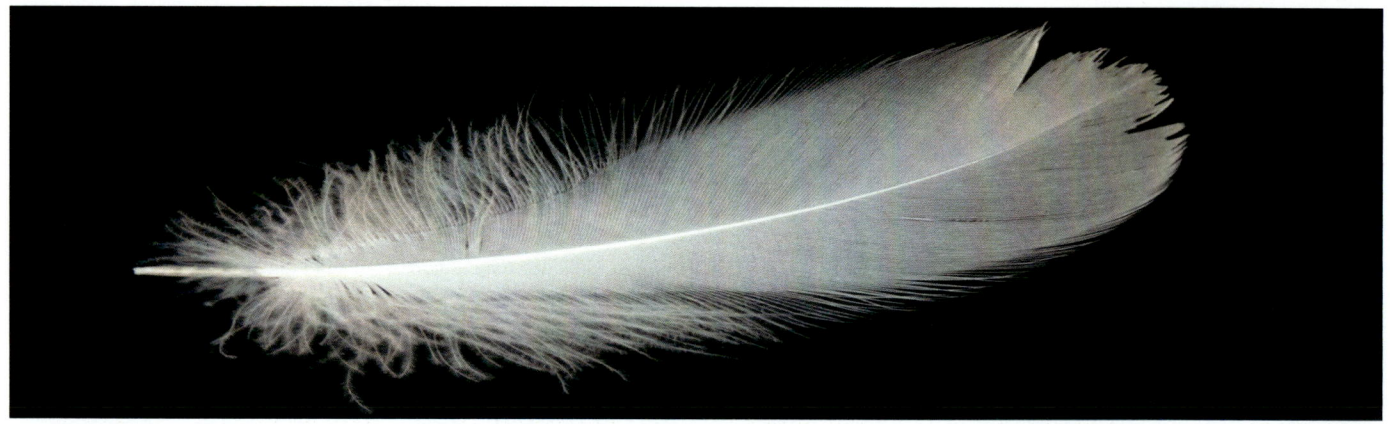

Resource 3a: things to think and talk about

1. Which passages in the portrait of Harry Stanton tell us something about the kind of person he was? Underline these parts of the text.
2. What is your opinion of the way the conscientious objectors were treated by the authorities? Think of both positives and negatives.
3. How hard do you think it was to stand out against public opinion? Why do you think so many people were intolerant of the pacifists?
4. How far do you agree with Harry that he should not only refuse to fight, but should also refuse to do anything that released others to fight?
5. Do you think refusing to fight in a war is an easy or hard decision? Why?

More things to do
Ask your students to find out more about COs in World War I:

- Listen to the Imperial War Museums' 'Voices of the First World War' Podcast 37: Conscientious objection at http://tinyurl.com/CO-Podcast37

- Discuss the 'conscience clause': Harry Stanton and the No-Conscription Fellowship were successful in securing the conscience clause in British law – the first time the legal right to refuse to fight was recognised. In the event, conscientious objection was not defined, and there were many problems with the tribunal system. Nevertheless, ask your students if the conscience clause is something to be proud of.

- Watch the film about the CO Arthur Gardner, who became mayor of his town: https://tinyurl.com/cogardener (7 minutes). Ask your students what they think of Arthur becoming mayor?
  Why do they think Huddersfield may have been more accepting of the COs than many other places in Britain?

- To find out more about people working to support conscientious objectors, and for a world without war, see: www.wri-irg.org/en.

More things to do

- Watch *Voices of Conscience* – six short films of personal experiences of war, conscientious objection and peacemaking. The films allow ordinary people to tell their personal stories, accompanied by photographs and illustrations from the period. Each film lasts for less than five minutes – accessible for all ages but ideal for those aged 7 to 11. They are accompanied by teachers' notes, available in English or Welsh. To view the films at www.vimeo.com/channels/voicesofconscience.

- Quakers in Britain are seeking to 'reclaim' the white feather. Explore the dilemmas of five Quakers featured in *The white feather diaries*, an online storytelling project to mark the centenary of World War I. The real-time story follows five Quakers as the war unfolds, with each exploring different choices in a daily blog and Twitter feed. The stories chart the individuals' journey of discovery as they find out that opposing war is not easy: www.whitefeatherdiaries.org.uk.

- Discuss how it might have felt to receive a white feather. Read 'My "coward" grandfather' below to explore this with your students. Ask your students if it was brave or cowardly to be a conscientious objector.

"*My grandfather's attempt to volunteer was turned down in 1914 because he was short-sighted. But in 1916, as he walked home to south London from his office, a woman gave him a white feather (an emblem of cowardice). He enlisted the next day. By that time, they cared nothing for short sight. They just wanted a body to stop a shell, which Rifleman James Cutmore duly did in February 1918, dying of his wounds on March 28.*

My mother was nine, and never got over it. In her last years, in the 1980s, her once fine brain so crippled by dementia that she could not remember the names of her children, she could still remember his dreadful, useless death. She could still talk of his last leave, when he was so shellshocked he could hardly speak and my grandmother ironed his uniform every day in the vain hope of killing the lice. She treasured his letters from the front, as well as information about his brothers who also died.

She blamed the politicians. She blamed the generation that sent him to war. She was with Kipling: 'If any question why we died, / Tell them, because our fathers lied.' She was with Sassoon: 'If I were fierce, and bald, and short of breath / I'd live with scarlet Majors at the Base, / And speed glum heroes up the line to death [...] And when the war is done and youth stone dead / I'd toddle safely home and die – in bed.'

But most of all, she blamed that unknown woman who gave him a white feather."

Francis Beckett, ***The Guardian***, 11 November 2008

Student resource 4: Women and families in World War I

At the time of World War I no women were allowed in the armed forces but there were many ways in which they could support the war effort, if they wished. Many young women without children went to work in the factories doing work previously done by the men.

Some women who had belonged to the suffragette movement stopped their 'votes for women' campaign and supported the war effort. They hoped that this would show they were responsible citizens and deserved the vote.

However, many suffragettes joined the peace movement and campaigned against the war. Women were key leaders in the No-Conscription Fellowship (NCF). Its organiser, Catherine Marshall, who had worked to achieve women's suffrage through peaceful and legal means, brought her experience, skills and political knowledge to the NCF. To resist the military system and win release, imprisoned conscientious objectors (COs) often used the suffragist technique of hunger strikes. For helping COs, Catherine reckoned she was technically liable to 2,000 years in prison. To learn more about her visit www.spartacus-educational.com/WmarshallCAT.htm.

The Women's Peace Crusade had over 100 branches across Britain. It organised street protests, public meetings and marches, and sold badges and gave out leaflets. One demonstration in Glasgow involved 14,000 people. It attracted many women whose husbands and sons had been killed in the war. Children carried banners with slogans such as "I want my Daddy". Women involved were often attacked at their meetings and in the press.

Many young women signed up as nurses to help the war effort. There were medical corps in the army but, as with the men, those who joined the Friends Ambulance Unit (FAU) were not subject to military law. This meant they were able to offer medical care to anyone in need, whether 'friend or foe'.

One woman who joined the Friends Ambulance Unit was Rachel Wilson, who came from Kidderminster. She was sent to serve at a hospital near Dunkirk run by the FAU. The strain of working close to the battleground and with badly wounded people shows in her diary entries. This one is from 21 March 1918:

"I was sitting comfortably before the firing [began] surveying the prospect of beginning work again when the sound of guns close to

Rachel Wilson with some of her colleagues. She is at the back, second from the right.

made me automatically spring from my chair and turn out the light. The firing continued and the cow [a siren] chimed in. The patients of course woke up and informed me it was a naval bombardment we were in for this time. [...] The noise was deafening and one could hear the shells whizzing through the air while the boom of our guns made a background of sound. I sat on one of the beds and chatted with the patients and longed for one moment of quiet to give my head a rest. After a bit I groped my way to the door and looked out at the blue glare of light outside. After about ten minutes the cracking and whizzing of the shells died down and only a more distant booming could be heard."

The noise had been coming from a naval battle in the English Channel. Shortly after, ten casualties arrived from the British destroyer *Botha*. Rachel learned that the *Botha* had rammed and sunk a German torpedo boat and then in the confusion had been torpedoed by a French destroyer. Rachel's diary records that all the men survived.

Life could also be very hard for the wives and families of conscientious objectors (COs). They often became social outcasts and lost many of their friends. Sometimes they were even rejected by their own families. Edith Peet was married to Hubert, who was a Quaker and a journalist. They had two small children called Mary and Joan. When Hubert refused to join up he was sent to prison as a CO. Edith wrote to Hubert saying that her parents and friends were finding it very difficult to understand why he had taken this stand. She wrote:

> "May God give you the strength to go on for it is the only way. You know that I stand with you and [...] back you up. If only I could do a little to help these children of ours to be more ready and fitted to fill their place in the world as worthily as their father is filling his I shall be thankful."

Hubert realised he had left his wife and two daughters in a very difficult situation. One day he sat down and wrote a letter to Mary and Joan to explain why he was in prison:

> "The English People and the German People have got angry with each other like two children who want the same toys, and hundreds of men are now trying to kill each other. Now Daddy and Mummy and lots of other people think it is wrong even if another person gets angry with you, for you to get angry with them. [...] This is why your Daddy says he cannot be a soldier and go and try and kill the daddies of little German boys and girls. Most people think he ought to go and, because he will not and he thinks it is wrong, they are shutting him up in prison."

Mary and Joan were not entirely convinced. Edith wrote shortly after that:

> "Mary stands up for you very much but I heard Joan say to her the other day, 'I think Daddy ought to have gone and been a soldier when they wanted him to go, Mary.' 'I don't,' said Mary very promptly."

It must have been very hard for parents to see their children suffer because of the stand they themselves were taking.

Resource 4a:
things to think and talk about

1. What qualities of character does it take to do what Rachel Wilson did? Do you agree or disagree with her that she should help enemy wounded as well as those of the allies?
2. What qualities of character does Edith Peet display?
3. Describe the hardships encountered by the wives and families of conscientious objectors. To what extent do you think COs were right to ask them to go through this?
4. Why do you think Joan Peet wasn't entirely convinced by the reasons her dad gave for his being in prison?

More things to do

Ask your students what images come to mind when they think about war and fighting. Images are often of the weapons and soldiers – largely images of men. How does war affect the lives of women and children today?

Key facts: girls and conflict

- There are 200 million girls in countries that are at risk of, in the midst of, or emerging from armed conflict.

- There are 100,000 girls among the estimated 300,000 child soldiers in the world today.

- More than half of the 39 million children out of school and living in countries affected by conflict are girls.

- Although the number of children out of school is falling, a disproportionate number of girls remain unable to attend school.

- Thousands of girls and young women – no-one knows exactly how many – have suffered rape and sexual abuse in times of war. Today, rape is used as a deliberate tactic in ethnic or religious conflicts.

"UN Security Council Resolution 1325 calls for the rights of women and girls in armed conflict to be protected and for their active participation in conflict prevention, peace processes and post-conflict reconstruction. Sadly, this is often not the reality experienced by girls and young women in conflict."
Graça Machel, international advocate for women's and children's rights

"Children do not start wars. Yet they are most vulnerable to its deadly effects. Millions of innocent children die in conflicts, which is no fault of theirs, just because some greedy leaders rob powers with the barrel of the gun. During such times everything freezes: no education, no drinking water, no electricity, food shortages, no shelter, and most of all some girls are raped, leading to HIV/AIDS."
Girl (17), Ghana

For more information visit www.becauseiamagirl.org.

For more information on the issue of child soldiers and the impact of conflict see www.child-soldiers.org.uk.

Explore the role of women in WWI with this QPSW resource: https://tinyurl.com/womenWW1.

A group of female workers seen beside the circular saws they operated in the Royal Gun Factory in the Royal Arsenal, Woolwich, London, in May 1918. © IWM – Image Ref: 27845

Student resource 5: Corder Catchpool, pacifist and 'bridge-builder'

Corder Catchpool was born in 1883, so he was over 30 when World War I broke out. He was a Quaker and a firm pacifist by the time he left school. He was an excellent footballer and had been captain of the teams in both of his secondary schools. His ambition was to become a doctor in order to help people. However, the cost of training was too great, so he became an engineer instead. He worked at first on the Great Eastern Railway, though he did not find this fulfilling. He then tried to work his way through medical school but found that the strain on his health was simply too great. He went back to engineering and became involved in building a garden village for the factory workers of Darwen in Lancashire.

At the start of the war, no one was forced to join the armed forces. Corder did not wish to fight but still felt very strongly that he had to do something useful. He felt that he could not be a 'bystander'. Corder decided that he would join the Friends Ambulance Unit (FAU), which was being formed by a group of Quakers. The FAU would allow pacifists to help anyone in need of medical aid, no matter whose side they fought on. If he had joined the Royal Army Medical Corps (RAMC) he would only have been able to treat British or Allied soldiers.

Because of his interest in medicine, Corder no doubt enjoyed the training given at a special camp set up at Jordans, a village in Buckinghamshire. It included stretcher drill, first aid and dressing practice. Then he and many others were ready to set sail for France. When they landed at Dunkirk they were met by a tide of wounded soldiers coming back from the front, waiting near the railway line. Corder wrote:

> "I shall never in my life forget the sight and sounds that met us. Figure two huge goods sheds, semi-dark, every inch of floor-space [...] covered with the flimsy French stretchers, and on each stretcher a wounded man, desperately wounded nearly every one. The air heavy with the stench of putrid flesh, and thick with groans and cries. Four hundred wounded, and one French medical student to attend to them, two English officers helping voluntarily. Half dead as we were with fatigue, we flung ourselves into this work throughout the night, the need was so great."

They worked all day, had a brief rest and then Corder asked permission to go back to the sheds again for the night, despite being exhausted. However, his officer refused – saying Corder needed to rest. Corder thought he was being heartless.

Before long, the Germans introduced a new weapon – gas – which choked and poisoned the soldiers. The casualties were very heavy, and Corder wrote:

> "The poor, choking, gasping, dying [...] beggars were already beginning to pour in. [...] the battle raged for five days and five nights before it began to abate. [...] Periodically, they shelled the village. We ran the gauntlet[10] until one driver was wounded and two cars put out of action. [...] Still we worked and flung ourselves down now and then for a brief sleep."

In 1915 Corder was asked to become an officer of the Friends Ambulance Unit, though he wanted to stay working closely with the wounded. Then, in 1916, conscription was finally introduced. This led to another battle of conscience for Corder. He thought that being in a medical corps might be seen as an easy way out for those who did not wish to fight. So he resigned from the FAU, returned to England and became a conscientious objector (CO). As with other COs, he came before a tribunal. They accepted his sincere objections to fighting but could not understand why he would not join the Royal Army Medical Corps. But Corder refused and was sent to prison with hard labour. He spent over two years in prison. Much of this was in solitary confinement.

Whilst in prison, Corder realised that it was not enough for him simply to refuse to take part in war. He had to do something positive for peace. So he began to learn German, and when the war was finally over he travelled to Germany to take part in Quaker relief work. Things were desperate and very many Germans were starving. In this way, Corder hoped he could help mend relations between the enemy countries and reduce the risk of such a war ever happening again.

Corder met his wife, Gwen, during the relief work in Germany just after the war. Back home in Darwen, he and Gwen started a family and were happy. They encouraged people to make contact with Germans. For example, every year they took parties of people from the local cotton mills out to Germany to try to build friendship and understanding.

Unfortunately, the conditions imposed on the Germans by the Allies after the war were very harsh. Many people believe they helped to create the circumstances that led to the rise of the German National Socialists (Nazis) in the 1930s.

In 1930 Corder was invited to work for the Quakers in Berlin. It needed some thought but Corder and Gwen accepted the challenge. This was a very difficult time in Germany, with Adolf Hitler coming to power in 1933. All the time, Corder tried to build bridges. Eventually, things became too dangerous for Corder's family and they all came back to England in 1936. But Corder never gave up his personal mission to build peace and friendship between nations. Corder defined an absolutist as "A man to whom the sinfulness of war seems so appalling that he must struggle against it, wrestle to deliver a world bound by it; feels that anything less would be to him drifting with the tide – not stemming it."

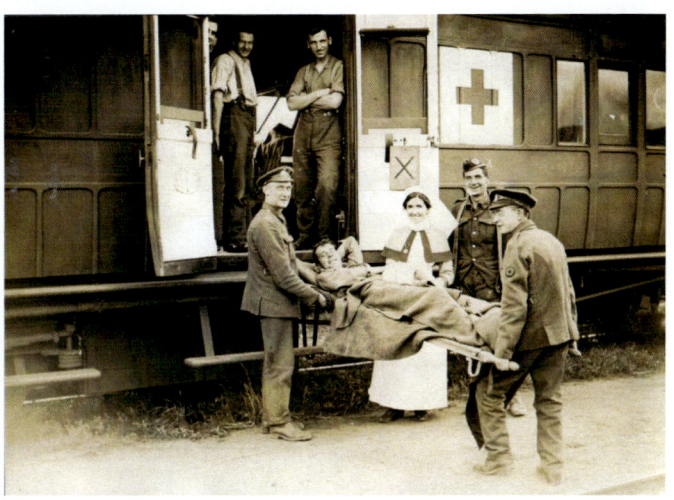

Friends Ambulance Unit members loading casualties onto ambulance train 17.

Not forgotten
During World War II, Leonhard Friedrich, a German Quaker refused to cooperate with the Nazis. Leonhard was taken off to Buchenwald concentration camp and suffered greatly. His health became very poor. But he was eventually helped by a Nazi officer who remembered being helped by the Quakers after World War I. He had been a small boy at that time. The officer found Leonhard an office job and because of this he was able to survive his ordeal.

Resource 5a:
things to think and talk about

1. Which passages in the portrait of Corder Catchpool tell us something about the kind of person he was? Underline these parts of the text.
2. To what extent do you agree with Corder's decision to join the Friends Ambulance Unit as opposed to a) fighting, and b) joining the Royal Army Medical Corps?
3. Corder was a Christian (a Quaker) and a pacifist, but most Christians agreed with the use of force in World War I. Why do you think this was? (See Information sheet 2: Is it ever right to fight in a war?) Where do you stand on this issue?
4. What do you think of Corder's refusal to stay in the Friends Ambulance Unit after conscription?
5. Some people would have thought that Corder's decision to go to Germany after the war was wrong. Why might they have thought that? What do you think Corder's motives were and what is your own view of his actions?
6. Corder told the court martial that sentenced him "I have heard a call above the roar of the guns". What do you think he meant by this?

More things to do
Ask your students to find out more about conscientious objection today.

What happens to members of the armed forces in Britain today who develop a 'conscientious objection'?

- To find out more about joining and leaving the army, do the quiz at www.beforeyousignup.info or see https://dontjointhearmy.co.uk.

- Research the case of Joe Glenton, the first British soldier to publicly refuse to go to Afghanistan: "It's not like you make a choice to be a conscientious objector… It's something that develops over time and goes against the grain of your being". See https://tinyurl.com/joeglentonvfp.

- Joe Glenton is a member of an organisation called 'Veterans for Peace'. Find out more about why former soldiers have joined this organisation at www.veteransforpeace.org.uk.

Some of the young men who took part in the first training camp for volunteers to the FAU.

Joe Glenton, former soldier and a member of Veterans for Peace, UK.

More things to do

Discuss the case of Omar Sa'ad, a conscientious objector repeatedly sent to prison for his refusal to join the Israeli Army. Watch a clip from Israel Social TV and listen to Omar Sa'ad explaining his reasons for refusing conscription at http://tinyurl.com/l6fwvlk.

- Omar Sa'ad, from a town in northern Israel, belongs to the Palestinian Arab Druze community. He opposes the idea of conscription by law for members of his community because it forces them to fight against their Arab brothers.

- From 2012 to 2014 Omar was sentenced seven times (150 days imprisonment) for his refusal to fight. Civilian lawyers were not allowed to visit Omar during his imprisonment. The army claims that civilian lawyers are not certified to enter military prisons. Omar issued a public statement: "...I declare it again and loudly: I am Omar Sa'ad Zaher Aldeen. I refuse to serve in the Israeli military army and I demand the respect for my faith and not to be obliged to do things that contradict with my conscience and principles. I want my freedom."

- In June 2014 the Israeli authorities officially released Omar from his military service, although they did not recognise his status as a conscientious objector. Unfortunately, being released can still have major consequences, as military service is an expectation of many employers.

Conscientious objection around the world. Thousands of COs today are in prison in South Korea, Israel, Finland, Spain, and many other countries. Find out more about the treatment of COs today at www.ppu.org.uk/coproject/cotoday.html.

- Article 18 of the Universal Declaration of Human Rights reads: "Everyone has the right to freedom of thought, conscience and religion". Whilst this does not explicitly refer to a right to conscientious objection, the United Nations Human Rights Committee believes that "such a right can be derived from article 18, inasmuch as the obligation to use lethal force may seriously conflict with the freedom of conscience and the right to manifest one's religion or belief". However, the legal definition and status of conscientious objection has varied over the years and from nation to nation.

Omar Sa'ad, a Palestinian-Druze conscious objector, talks before his family members and supporters.
© 2013 Oren Ziv/Activestills.org

Student resource 6: Henry Williamson, the nature-loving soldier

Henry as a young soldier in 1915.

Henry Williamson was born in London in 1895. By the time World War I broke out he was 18 and had found a job as a clerk in an insurance office. He was clever but did not want to go to university. At school he had been a good runner. He had also joined the Scout movement and the school rifle association. Most of all he loved nature and was fond of riding his bike into the country to collect birds' eggs (this was not illegal in those days).

In 1914 the clouds of war were beginning to form and Henry decided to join the London Rifle Brigade (LRB) as a part-time volunteer. Henry thought he would be on defensive duties in England if war broke out. However, shortly after the fighting began in August, the LRB was sent for training for a month or two before setting sail for France. Henry realised that, once his brigade started fighting, many of them would die. In a letter home he wrote:

29 August 1914

"You must not mind my going abroad. [...] It is probable that if LRB does go (and we shall be needed against those never ending masses) abroad, that about one fifth will return alive. The others will join their comrades in the deep, deep sleep. Still, I must not alarm you. I have volunteered because I know you want me to help the allies in my best manner."

Henry often enquired about his friends and relations and reminded his parents about looking after his birds' eggs. At the same time he was thinking about why he had decided to fight:

19 September 1914

"Those gulls eggs in the cupboard which are not blown must be burnt, but please don't burn the Buzzards eggs if by any chance they are there. The gulls eggs are some of them blown with a hole in them, so lock them in my drawer. [...] I am afraid this war will mean the ruin (financially and otherwise) and break-up of many English families. Be sure that if I go abroad, I will fight like a devil and a Williamson against these barbarians who are doing the Fiends[11] own hellish work in wrecking the peace of Europe, and causing grief and anguish in millions of homes. A chap here who lost his son in the war cursed them, and it was terrible to hear. I feel the same at times, and if there ever is a bayonet charge I will be one of the first to stab and thrust at them. [...] Put up the bird boxes in Feb for the tomtits."

11. The Fiend is another name for the Devil.

Henry's brigade sailed for France on 4 November 1914. The Germans were already in control of most of Belgium. They had crossed into France and were quite close to Paris. It was not long before Henry's brigade was close to the front near a Belgian village called Ploegsteert (which they nicknamed Plug Street). This was just a few kilometres from Lille across the border in France (see map). The war was beginning to change from open fighting to trench warfare, in which neither side was able to gain much ground without great effort and loss of life. Also, the weather was wet and miserable. The men spent a lot of time digging and repairing trenches. They were able to take breaks from the trenches in order to rest. Henry wrote home about what his life was like:

> "It has been awful in the trenches. For two days and nights we have been in nearly 36 inches of mud & water. Can you picture us sleeping standing up, cold and wet half way up to our thighs, and covered in mud. As we crept into the trenches at dead of night over 1 foot of mud, the Germans sent up Magnesium flares, and we had to crouch flat while scores of bullets spat amongst us. [...] My feet are now twice their normal size, and I have such rheumatism in my right leg that it is agony to move. [...] A Corporal & I waited 1 hour for a sniper, & I had the pleasure to shoot him in the end. Otherwise we practically never see a German. Altho' we are entrenched within 100 yards of their trenches."

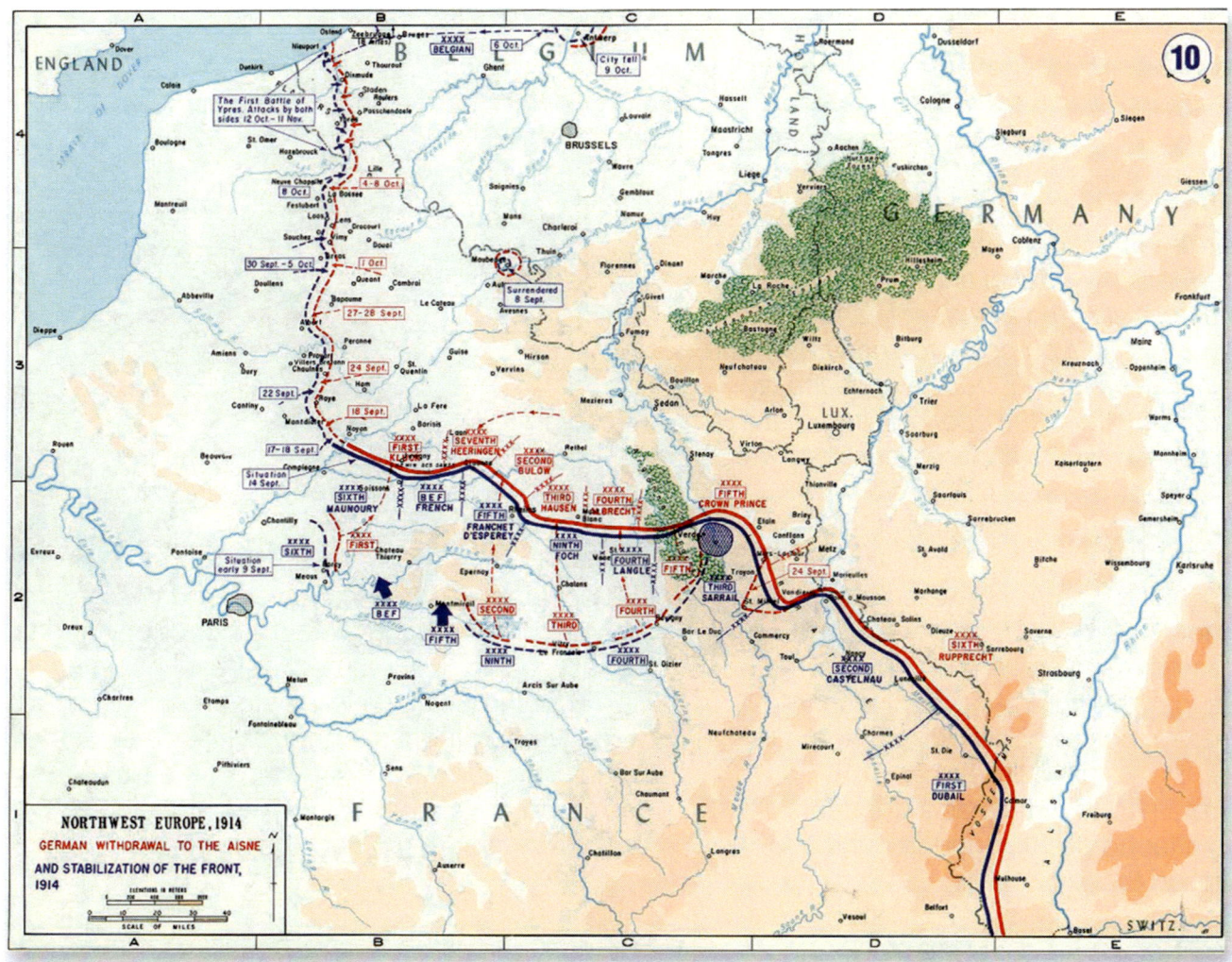

Map of the Western Front, 1914

33

And so things went on, with neither side being able to advance any distance. Then on Christmas Eve something extraordinary happened. This was how Henry described it in a letter he wrote home on Boxing Day 1914:

> "On Xmas eve both armies sang carols and cheered & there was very little firing. The Germans (in some places 80 yds away) called to our men to come & fetch a cigar & our men told them to come to us. This went on for some time, neither fully trusting the other, until, after much promising to 'play the game' a bold Tommy[12] crept out & stood between the trenches, & immediately a Saxon[13] came to meet him. They shook hands & laughed & then 16 Germans came out. Thus the ice was broken. Our men are speaking to them now. [...] Many are gentle looking men in goatee beards and spectacles, and some are very big and arrogant looking. I have some cigarettes which I shall keep, & a cigar I have smoked. We had a burial service in the afternoon, over the dead Germans who perished in the 'last attack that was repulsed against us'. The Germans put 'For Fatherland and Freedom' on the cross. They obviously think their cause is a just one."

He then goes on to talk about his swollen feet and his frostbitten toes. Henry's daughter-in-law later wrote that Henry

"...could never forget what he learned that day – that the German soldiers thought as deeply and sincerely as the English that they were fighting for God and their country. [...] As time passed his thoughts about the causes of war deepened and hardened. He saw that war was created by greed, misplaced zeal and bigotry. [...] All these factors affected him deeply and came to determine his life's purpose; to show the world, through his writing, that truth and peace lay solely in beauty and the open air, and that this was the only way to avoid a repetition of war."

It was not long after Boxing Day that Henry became ill with a stomach complaint called enteritis, along with a very severe case of 'trench foot'. He became very weak and was taken back to England on 26 January 1915. He was looked after in Ancoats Hospital, Manchester, before being allowed home to recover. It was not until February 1917 that Henry returned to France as a transport officer looking after horses that carted guns and ammunition to the front line.

Note
Unlike many of his friends and comrades, Henry Williamson survived the war. However, it left a deep mark on him. He was a keen lover of nature before he enlisted, and when he became a writer and novelist the two great themes of his writing were the horror of war and an appreciation of nature. His best known novel is *Tarka the Otter*, which is still in print and is widely thought of as a popular classic. It was made into a film in 1974. A clip of the film can be found on YouTube at www.youtube.com/watch?v=mjnSAATCOoc.

12. A nickname for a British soldier.
13. A Saxon is a German from the region of Saxony, which is near the Czech and Polish borders.

Resource 6a: things to think and talk about

1. Which passages in the portrait of Henry Williamson tell us something about the kind of person he was? Underline these parts of the text.
2. How does Henry describe the consequences of war for individuals and their families?
3. What can you gather about how Henry's attitudes to his enemy changed before and after the Christmas Truce? What led Henry to change his mind about war?
4. The Christmas Day Truce of 1914 has become very famous as an extraordinary incident that never happened again. Think and write about the feelings of individuals who lived through the ceasefire and who, just a few days later, were killing men they had recently made friends with.

More things to do

- Watch an interview with Henry Williamson in which he talks about life on the Western Front and the Christmas Truce of 1914 at www.bbc.co.uk/iplayer/episode/p01tcyg5/the-great-war-interviews-3-henry-williamson (30 minutes).

- Watch *Balls to war – when a world war stopped to play football* at www.noglory.org/index.php/balls-to-war-when-a-world-war-stopped-to-play-football (7 minutes).

- During the Christmas Truce the soldiers were surprised that 'the enemy' were just like them in so many ways. This was because of the kind of propaganda they'd been exposed to. During World War I, and in every other war, terrible lies are spread about the enemy and what they have done. Why do you think this is? Can they think of any groups of people the media treat as suspicious, or even spread lies about today? Discuss how groups can become 'othered' and how identities can be portrayed or perceived as one-dimensional (such as Muslims, Gypsies, travellers or asylum-seekers).

- What can be done to help break down barriers? Have you, or anyone you know, acted as an 'upstander' rather than a 'bystander' and reached out across a divide?

Facing History and Ourselves has lesson plans and activities to help further explore identity, such as 'Identity and Belonging in a Changing Great Britain': www.facinghistory.org/for-educators/educator-resources/resources/identity-and-belonging-changing-great-britain.

Bibliography

Boulton, David (1967). *Objection overruled.* London: MacGibbon & Kee.

Goodall, Felicity (2010). *We will not go to war: conscientious objection during the World Wars.* Stroud: The History Press.

Hochschild, Adam (2012). *To End All Wars: A Story of Loyalty and Rebellion, 1914–1918.* London: Pan.

Hughes, William R. (1964). *Indomitable Friend: Corder Catchpool 1883–1952.* London: Housmans.

Page 34 photo information: Officers and men of 26th Divisional Ammunition Train (Army Service Corps) playing football in Salonika, Christmas 1915. © IWM - Image Ref: 31576

Key terms and information sheets

Key terms

Absolutist
A conscientious objector who demanded absolute, or unconditional, exemption from military service, also known as an 'absolute pacifist'. Absolutists took the view that any compromise at all with the conscription system, even accepting organised civilian work, was to allow oneself to become a cog in the war machine. Many spent years in prison during and after World War I.

Alternativist
A conscientious objector who accepted (often reluctantly) exemption from military service conditional upon performing civilian 'work of national importance', often working on farms or in hospitals. Some Quakers and other religious conscientious objectors volunteered for the Friends Ambulance Unit. Other alternativists accepted the role of soldiers in the Non-Combatant Corps (NCC), assisting with transport and stores for food, clothing or helping to look after the roads or railways, but not carrying weapons. People who were willing to get involved in the war but refused to take up arms were also called 'relative' pacifists.

Conscientious objector (CO)
A conscientious objector is a person who "as a matter of conscience objects to combatant service". Individuals registering for exemption from military service during World War I had three options: (i) to serve in the Non-Combatant Corps or the Royal Army Medical Corps; (ii) to undertake alternative civilian service not under military control; or (iii) to claim absolute exemption. The grounds for objection varied: some, such as Quakers, objected on religious grounds, while others were opposed to the war on political grounds.

Conscription
When the military needs people to fight in a war, but there aren't enough volunteers, sometimes they'll begin conscription. This is a law that says if you are able to fight, you have to fight. In Britain the Military Service Act came into force in March 1916. This imposed conscription on all single men aged between 18 and 41, but exempted the medically unfit, clergymen, teachers and certain classes of industrial worker. Conscientious objectors could also apply for exemption. Conscription was later extended to married men in June 1916, and the upper age limit was raised to 51 in 1918.

Friends Ambulance Unit (FAU)
World War I began on 4 August 1914. Meeting for Sufferings (the key policy body for Quakers in Britain) met in London three days later to consider its response. A group of young Quakers came up with the idea of an ambulance unit. They were convinced that ambulance services would be terribly inadequate and that offering such services could save many lives. It would also enable conscientious objectors to make a vital contribution. There was no conscription then, so none of them had to get involved – their response came from their commitment to participating in a nonviolent way. Although unarmed, many members of the FAU joined armies in the field (sometimes dangerously close to the front lines) in order to provide humanitarian assistance to those affected by the war.

Human rights
Human rights are fundamental rights that belong to every person simply because he or she is a human being. They are based on the principle that every human being is born equal in dignity and rights. All human rights are equally important and they cannot be taken away under any circumstances. They are important because they protect our right to live in dignity. This means that we should have things such as a decent place to live and

enough to eat. It means we should be able to participate in society, to receive an education, to work, to practise our religion, to speak our own language, and to live in peace. Human rights are a tool to protect people from violence and abuse. The Universal Declaration of Human Rights (UDHR) is the founding document of human rights. Adopted on 10 December 1948 by the United Nations, the UDHR stands as a common reference point for the world and sets common standards of achievement in human rights.

Just war
A war that is considered 'just', or right. For more on 'just war theory' see Information sheet 2.

Mediator
A mediator is someone who supports others to resolve disputes or conflicts by helping them to find a 'win-win' solution. A mediator never takes sides, but instead helps all participants to reach a solution they are happy with. Mediation is voluntary and must be agreed to by all parties. It is confidential (unless there are safety or legal issues) and focuses on the future by looking forward positively.

No-Conscription Fellowship (NCF)
An organisation formed to support conscientious objectors in World War I, the NCF opposed the campaign to bring in conscription in 1916 because it considered human life to be sacred. The NCF was unsuccessful in opposing conscription, but it successfully fought for a law allowing people to opt out of fighting on grounds of conscience, known as the 'conscience clause'. The NCF then kept careful records of every CO, the grounds of his objection, his appearances before tribunals and courts, and even which prison he was held in. It also maintained contact with COs, arranging visits to camps, barracks and prisons across the country. The NCF had its own press department that continuously sought to draw the public's attention to what was happening to COs, particularly the ill-treatment and brutality many were subjected to.

Nonviolence
The word 'nonviolence' is understood in different ways. Many people take it to mean simply 'not violent' and see it as a gentle, harmless, non-confrontational approach. For some, nonviolence is associated with 'people power', using the power of demonstrations or non-cooperation to change a situation. In this sense it is a useful and effective tactic. For others, the word describes something about the ultimate goal of nonviolent action: it brings together the nature of the action with the spirit of love from which it springs. For them, nonviolence has a deeper dimension, which might be spiritual or religious. For more on nonviolence see Information sheet 2.

Pacifism
Pacifists believe that war and violence are unjustifiable. For Quakers, pacifism not only means the refusal to fight, it also encompasses a duty to remove the causes of war and to actively work for peace.

Quaker
A member of the Religious Society of Friends, founded by George Fox in the 17th century. Quakers share a way of life rather than a fixed set of beliefs. Quaker worship is based on silent waiting, in which they expect to come into the presence of God. The stillness gives space and time to reflect and think. An important Quaker belief is that there is "that of God in everyone",[14] which means that everyone is special and unique. Quaker beliefs and practices have their origins in Christianity, but Quakers also find inspiration and value in the teachings of other faiths. Quakers think that peace, equality, truth, simplicity and sustainability are all important ideals to work towards.

Remembrance
Remembrance Day is observed on 11 November each year, and Remembrance Sunday is held on the second Sunday in November, the one closest to this date. Many people wear poppies as 11 November draws near. But why 11 November? At the 11th hour of the 11th day of the 11th month in 1918 the

---

14. *Advices & queries* 17, Yearly Meeting of the Religious Society of Friends (Quakers) in Britain, 2008.

guns fell silent. The killing stopped. This was the armistice – the agreement to end the fighting. After the war people wanted to mark the event on a special day, so they chose Armistice Day. Today, in addition to Remembrance Sunday, many people observe a minute or two of silent reflection at 11am on 11 November, no matter what day of the week it falls on.

Tribunal
A tribunal is a kind of court. If you wanted to be a CO during World War I you had to apply to a tribunal, which involved a panel of people listening to your arguments. If you could prove that you were a member of a religious group like the Quakers, you were more likely to be believed. If you were not believed, you were ordered to enlist or go to prison. A major problem faced by COs in World War I was that tribunals were composed of local people and always included someone from the military whose job it was to demolish their case. No one spoke up on their behalf. There was no prosecution and defence. There was only prosecution. This was not a fair system and was improved for COs in World War II.

Information sheet 1: How did World War I start?

The build-up to the outbreak of World War I is a tale of major European empires trying to maintain or increase their power and weaken the threats from their rivals.

The key players were the Austro-Hungarian Empire, the German Empire, The Ottoman Empire (which was Turkish and based in Istanbul), Russia and the British Empire. Britain at that time was the largest of all the world powers.

Around the year 1900 the Balkans (including Serbia, Bosnia, Macedonia and Bulgaria) was a very unstable area. It had been under the control of the Ottoman Empire, but in 1909 Austria-Hungary took over Bosnia. This angered many Serbians, who wanted to be independent and free.

Meanwhile, the German Empire, under Kaiser Wilhelm II, was building up its own power. This was in order to rival the British Empire. The Germans also wanted to keep the French in a weak state and also to keep Russia pushed back away from its own borders. Germany had an alliance with Austria-Hungary, its close neighbour. To counter this, Britain entered into agreements with Russia and France to provide support for each other if necessary.

On 28 June 1914 the heir to the throne of Austria-Hungary, Archduke Franz Ferdinand, was shot during a visit to Sarajevo in Bosnia. His killer was a Serbian student called Gavrilo Princip. This triggered a series of events that led to the outbreak of war on a global scale. Austria-Hungary, supported by Germany, declared war on Serbia on 28 July.

Russia then moved in support of its neighbour, Serbia, and called on France for support. In response, Germany declared war on Russia on 1 August. The Germans also decided to invade France, hoping to weaken it quickly before concentrating on Russia. Unfortunately, to get to France the Germans would have to go through Belgium, which was neutral. The Belgians refused to allow the Germans to pass through their country, so the Germans decided to invade Belgium.

Although Britain's agreement with France did not oblige it to go to war, there was an earlier treaty, signed by all the European powers in 1839, guaranteeing that Belgium should remain neutral. This treaty obliged Britain to defend Belgium if necessary. So when Germany invaded Belgium, Britain demanded that Germany withdraw its troops or face the consequences. The Germans ignored these demands, so on 4 August 1914 Britain entered the war.

Who or what was to blame for the outbreak of war? This was a time when countries like Britain and Germany were gaining huge wealth from their control of countries around the world, including in Africa. And Russia was keen to gain control of the areas around Istanbul so that its ships could sail through the Black Sea into the Mediterranean Sea. Large nations were often jealous and wary of each other, and many smaller countries saw the war as a chance to be free and independent.

One expert on the war put it like this: "The fundamental causes of the conflict can be epitomised in three words – fear, hunger, pride".[15]

---

15. BH Liddell Hart, *History of the First War*, London: Pan Books Ltd., 1972. Page 18.

Information sheet 2: Is it ever right to fight in a war?

Think about these two questions:

- Is violence a good thing?

- Would it ever be right to use violence?

You can probably see that these questions are similar but different. And the difference is very important. Most people would surely say that violence is never a good thing in itself. Violence causes harm, injury, misery, and creates victims, so someone is always worse off. Also, violence comes from negative feelings such as anger, hatred, revenge, or from a thirst for power and a wish to control others.

But what about the question, "Would it ever be right to use violence?"? Many people would answer, "It might be right if it prevented even worse violence or stopped some other form of injustice." For example, if someone steps in and uses force to prevent an innocent person being attacked, it could be argued that in this case the force is justified. It is not good but it is better than leaving a victim at the mercy of an attacker. Another way of putting this is that stepping in is 'the lesser of two evils'. Perhaps it is even a moral duty.

But even if the violence is 'justified', is it still okay if the person stepping in goes on to deliberately kill the attacker? It is probably fair to argue that this would be 'over the top', or out of proportion (disproportionate) and wrong.

In a similar way, people have for centuries debated whether it is ever right to fight in a war. Most of the major world religions preach love and peace, including Christianity, Islam, Sikhism and Buddhism, and the importance of forgiveness. Christians, for example, are told to love their enemies and do good to those who harm them. And one of the Ten Commandments is 'Do not kill'.

On this basis, most people would say that a war that was started to gain power or wealth, or out of greed or hatred, is not morally right. However, if, for example, a strong country invaded a weaker country in order to take it over, would it be right for a third country to go to war to protect the weaker country? Opinions vary as to the right answer to this question. Some argue that fighting in self-defence or to protect a weaker country can be justified on certain conditions. Others, a minority, argue that war can never be justified under any conditions – these people are called 'absolute pacifists' or 'absolutists'.

The 'just war' position

The arguments that set out the conditions under which a war might be justified are known as 'just war theory'. They were developed over the centuries, beginning with the Christian philosophers Augustine of Hippo and Thomas Aquinas, to define when it's right to go to war and the fairest ways to conduct war. In more detail, just war theory says that a war is justified:

- if the violence is a last resort and every way of resolving the problem by peaceful means has failed

- if it prevents greater violence or a greater injustice

- if it is proportionate and no unnecessary violence is used

- if the methods of warfare used are themselves 'reasonable' and in accordance with the 'rules of war'.

Of course, the decision about whether any particular war is 'just' depends on the situation. So even people who believe that war can sometimes be justified might disagree about a particular war or about whether the balance of the argument lies in favour or against.

The pacifist position

The pacifist position is based on principle. If violence is wrong, and the taking of life is wrong, then it follows that warfare is wrong. Nothing makes it right. In World War I many religious pacifists in the UK – including Quakers, Plymouth Brethren, Christadelphians and Jehovah's Witnesses – argued that they were following the teachings of Jesus in trying to love their enemies. Other pacifists – including those motivated by political beliefs – argued that wars are started by a country's leaders and that ordinary people should not be put in a position of killing other ordinary people because they did not start the war and do not deserve to die. International socialists, for example, believed that the working classes should refuse to obey the ruling classes because it is the ruling classes who always benefit at the expense of the working classes. Corder Catchpool believed that war was 'sinful', and nothing anyone could do to him would make him kill a fellow human being since we are all God's creatures. Harry Stanton believed that it was right to resist when the state was telling him to take human life. After all, if everyone did this, the war could not happen and a great deal of human suffering would be avoided.

Many Christian Churches adopt the just war position, but some have strong pacifist groups within them. Others have always maintained a strong pro-peace stance.

'Relative' and 'absolute' pacifists

During the war many pacifists refused to enlist, claiming that war was wrong. However, they agreed to take on 'non-combatant' roles, in other words work that did not involve fighting or killing. A good example would be the people who worked on the land or joined a medical corps. Many pacifists joined the Friends Ambulance Unit. It chose not to discriminate between 'friend' and 'foe' and treated anyone in need of medical help, regardless of which side they were on. Regular army ambulance units only treated their own wounded. People who are willing to get involved but refuse to take up arms are called 'relative pacifists'.

Some pacifists took the view that to do anything that might help the war effort, including any work (e.g. farming) that could release someone else to fight, was wrong. Such people are called 'absolute pacifists'.

Nonviolent resistance

Closely associated with pacifists are those who advocate nonviolent resistance. This is often known as 'civil disobedience'.

Nonviolent resistance is an approach that can be used by both pacifists and non-pacifists. Pacifists are nonviolent out of principle, but non-pacifists might use nonviolence because it can be the most effective method of protest. This is because it gives a government no excuse to squash a protest on the grounds of keeping order or protecting the peace. Peaceful resistance might be adopted by an unarmed group of civilians against an unjust government. Gandhi famously used nonviolent resistance against British rule in India. Gandhi's example had a great influence on the American civil rights movement led by Martin Luther King. It also influenced Nelson Mandela in his struggle against white rule in South Africa. Mandela, in his situation, eventually felt that nonviolence was ineffective against a brutal regime. The African National Congress (ANC) decided to use violence against state property, such as power lines. Despite being imprisoned for 27 years, when he was released Mandela realised that violence used against the white minority would draw South Africa into a bloodbath that would be catastrophic for both white and black people.

Information sheet 3: Conscription and conscientious objection

When war broke out in 1914 Britain already had an army of 85,000 men. In the first month of the war there was an appeal for volunteers, and in just one month over three-quarters of a million men volunteered – for a variety of reasons.

These included:

- patriotism – fighting to defend your family, your neighbours and your country

- propaganda – this made fighting sound brave, heroic and exciting. It also spread horrible rumours about the enemy that were often untrue

- peer pressure – when everyone else was joining up, it was hard to stand out and refuse. Groups of friends from the same street or town were allowed to join up together. Many people who refused to volunteer were called cowards and un-patriotic.

Many people believed that the war would be over by Christmas 1914, but it dragged on throughout 1915, with over a thousand soldiers killed every day. By 1916 hundreds of thousands of men had been killed or injured, and volunteers were drying up. The government decided that it would have to introduce conscription to force men to fight. So it passed a law requiring every fit man between the ages of 18 and 41 to enlist (see page 36). Later on in the war the upper age limit was raised to 51.

Members of the No-Conscription Fellowship (NCF) had opposed the campaign to bring in conscription because they believed all human life to be sacred. They were unsuccessful in this, but they also fought for a law allowing people to opt out of fighting on grounds of conscience. This became known as the 'conscience clause'.

After conscription was introduced most men obeyed the call-up. But 20,000 men said no and claimed that they were against fighting the war on principle – for them it was a matter of conscience. In most cases, these men objected for religious or political reasons. They were either following the commandment "Do not kill" and Jesus' teaching to love our enemies, or they were socialists who believed in the 'brotherhood of all men' (i.e. 'people'). Socialists believed that ordinary (working class) people around the world should refuse to fight wars started by the ruling classes for their own reasons. Men who refused to fight for such reasons of conscience were known as 'conscientious objectors', or COs.

If you wanted to be a CO you had to apply to a tribunal (a kind of court), which would listen to your arguments. If you could prove that you were a member of a religious group like the Quakers, you were more likely to be believed. If you were not believed, you were ordered to enlist or go to prison.

A major problem faced by COs in World War I was that tribunals were composed of local people and always included someone from the military whose job it was to demolish their case. No one spoke up on their behalf. There was no prosecution and defence. There was only prosecution. This was not a fair system and was improved for COs in World War II.

If you were believed, you were offered the chance to do something else for your country that did not involve killing, such as joining an army medical unit or the Friends Ambulance Unit. Otherwise you might be asked to work on the land producing much-needed food. Men who performed this work, as long as it was outside of military control, were known as 'alternativists'. Other COs were offered non-combatant roles in the army. Non-combatants joined the army, but only on condition that they were not trained to use or carry weapons.

Instead they carried out such duties as supplying the troops with what they needed or maintaining the roads and railway lines. Most COs accepted one of these options.

However, for some COs even the idea of doing something like farming was an indirect way of keeping the war going. And it might also release a farmhand to join up. They were known as 'absolutist' COs. Tribunals had the power to grant them complete exemption, but this rarely happened. In many cases their applications were turned down altogether, which meant that they could be called up as ordinary soldiers. If they then refused they could be arrested and handed over to the military; and if they disobeyed military orders they would be court-martialled and sent to prison. Likewise, when absolutists refused the offer of a non-combatant option, they were usually sent to prison. Prison often involved hard labour, solitary confinement, and physical and mental abuse. It is thought that 81 COs died as a result of their treatment in the army, prisons or 'work centres'.

In all, around 6,000 COs were imprisoned. Such a large number led to a scandal in the press and in Parliament, so in 1916 another option was introduced. Under the new Home Office Scheme COs would be released from prison and allowed to wear civilian clothes if they agreed to live in a work camp. They would also, under curfew, be allowed out of the camp in the evenings and on Sundays. There was a work camp near Aberdeen called Dyce, and Dartmoor Prison (renamed Princetown Work Centre in late 1916) also became one.

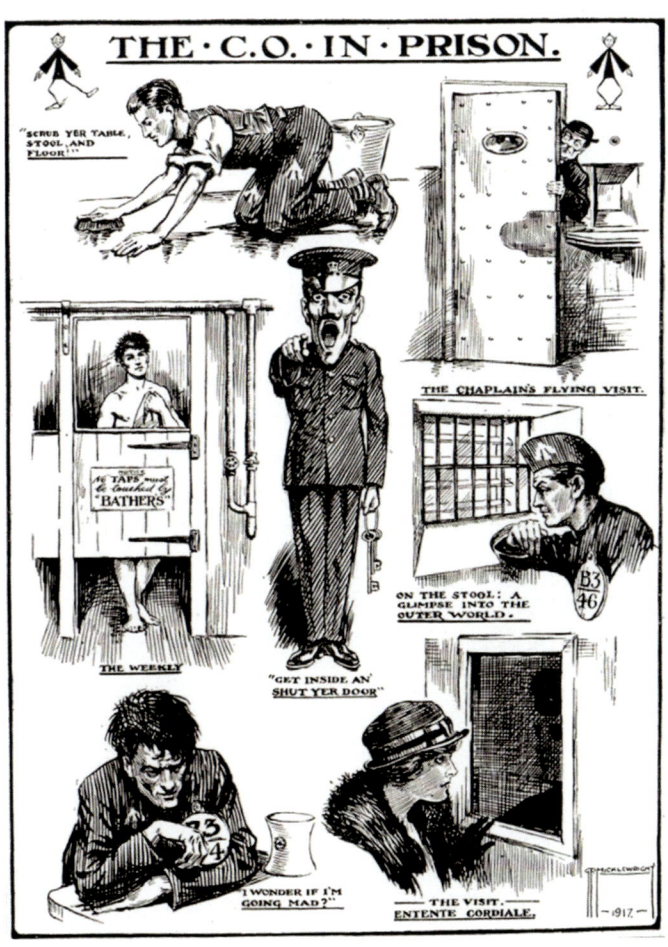

What a C.O. feels like. G.P. Mickelwright, 1917.

The C.O. in Prison. G.P. Mickelwright, 1917.

Further activities

Violence/war barometer

Create a line in your classroom, or draw a line on the board. Ask your students to place the characters they have learnt about along it, with those 'very keen to fight' at one end and those who 'won't fight or do anything to assist the war' at the other.

| Very keen to fight | Not keen to fight but must do something positive | Won't fight or do anything else that might assist the |

- Identify a space in the classroom where students can create a line or a 'U' shape. Place 'strongly agree' and 'strongly disagree' signs at opposite ends of a continuum in your room. Ask the students to consider the statement 'War is always wrong' and explain that they will be asked to place themselves along the line.

- Since this involves students literally putting themselves and their opinions on the line, emphasise the need to respect the opinions and voices of others, and call for them to be honest but not insulting. When offering their opinion or defence of their stance, ask students to use 'I' language, rather than 'You' language because this can be accusatory.

- Ask students to stand at the point on the line that represents their opinion, telling them that if they stand at either extreme they are absolute in their agreement or disagreement. They may also stand anywhere in between the two extremes, depending on how much they agree or disagree with the statement.

- Repeat the spectrum activity in relation to the question 'Is it ever right to fight?', asking the students to think about their own lives. Ask the students if there are ways of 'fighting' that are nonviolent? In their own lives, what might a nonviolent response to a nasty remark or put-down be? Can the students think of successful campaigns or movements that have used nonviolence to successfully struggle against oppression?

- Once the students have lined themselves up, ask them to explain why they have chosen to stand where they are. Encourage students to refer to evidence and examples when defending their stance. It is probably best to alternate from one end to the middle to the other end, rather than allowing too many voices from one stance to dominate. After about three or four viewpoints have been heard, ask if anyone wishes to move. Encourage students to keep an open mind – they are allowed to move if someone presents an argument that alters where they want to stand on the line. Run the activity until you feel most or all voices have been heard, making sure that no one person dominates.

- You may want to help the students debrief this exercise. You can have students reflect individually by writing about how the activity changed or reinforced their original opinion. Or you can chart the main 'for' and 'against' arguments on the board as a whole-class activity.

- To further explore the theme of nonviolence, show the students the film *Freedom Riders*. It shows the brave actions taken to dismantle the structures of discrimination in the Deep South of the United States in the 1960s. For more lesson ideas on nonviolence go to www.facinghistory.org/for-educators/educator-resources/lessons-and-units/nonviolence-tool-change.

- For a whole range of resources and materials to support teachers, trainers and community workers who want to build solidarity and cohesion, visit www.teachingforsolidarity.com.

- To explore nonviolence with young people see: https://tinyurl.com/youthrefusing.

Values mapping

- All the people featured in *Conviction* had dreams, values and many good principles. Ask the students where they think these values and beliefs came from.

- Ask the students where they think their own values come from. To explore this, have the students draw around one of their hands. On each finger they write a value that they hold – they need to think about things they feel strongly about.

- After writing these on the fingers of the hand (it's fine if they can only think of two or three), ask the students to draw over the hand again, in a different colour, and use this colour to write one inspiration for this value (they can write in the palm or outside of the hand). For example: 'not stealing' – Islam – I am a Muslim and the Qur'an says…; or 'women should be treated equally' – my mum – she looks after me on her own and works as well, she definitely deserves to be treated fairly…

Loyalty ranking

Responding to war is often a question of loyalty. Many pacifists were religious but many were not – they often believed in international socialism or the 'brotherhood of all mankind'.

- Show your students the piece of graffiti from Richmond Castle (Resource A). This is where 16 conscientious objectors were held in 1916 and wrote messages on the walls that remain there today. What do the students think of this view?

- Ask the students to make a hierarchy of their loyalty using the loyalty ranking sheet (Resource B). Photocopy this sheet for each student and cut out the cards. Students then rank their loyalty and present their decisions to a partner or small group.

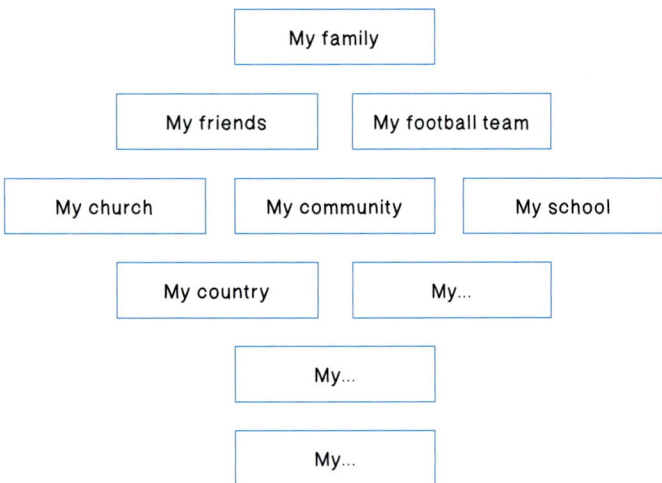

- Ask the students how their loyalties affect their views on war and violence. Which family members or personal experiences have influenced the views they hold?

Women and the British Army: research and discuss

Women are no longer banned from joining the British Army (as they were during World War I). Around 70 per cent of all posts in the army are open to women. They can find themselves on the front line serving as medics, intelligence specialists, artillery spotters, logisticians or signallers. However, the British Army's rules forbid the deployment of women in operations where they would be expected to "close with and kill the enemy". They remain barred from all infantry battalions and Royal Marine Commando units – including Special Forces – and from tank regiments and other armoured units. Ask the students why they think this is? Do they think this is fair?

Set up a debate on the following statement:

"The British Armed Forces should treat women the same as men – to do anything else is sexist."

Divide your class into two teams and get them to do some research about the facts. Ask them to have an example to back up their argument, from World War I as well as from the present day. Each side takes notes and asks questions after the speakers have made their case. Hold a vote at the beginning and end of the debate.

For an article on this issue go to www.theguardian.com/uk/defence-and-security-blog/2013/jan/24/reason-and-uk-and-army-and-women.

Mediation: role-play a conflict situation

Ask your students to work in groups of three. Each student is given one of the parts from the story *Big Grey and Little Red* (Resource C): the wolf (Big Grey), Little Red Riding Hood (Little Red) or the mediator.

When they have all read through the situation from their character's perspective, the mediator attempts to enable Big Grey and Little Red to share their feelings and, if possible, support them to find a way forward.

Allow time to debrief the role play. How did the students feel playing their character? Did they find the mediation useful? Which steps in this process do they think are particularly important or difficult? You may want to repeat the role-play with the students taking on different roles. Discuss with the students whether they use any of the aspects of the mediation process in their own lives.

Remembrance: how should we remember those who have died in past wars, and does remembrance glorify war?

- Remembrance Sunday is held "to commemorate the contribution of British and Commonwealth military and civilian servicemen and women in the two World Wars and later conflicts".[16] It is held on the second Sunday in November, which is the Sunday nearest to 11 November, or Armistice Day. The World War I armistice between the Allies and Germany took effect at the "11th hour of the 11th day of the 11th month" of 1918.

Remembrance Sunday is marked by ceremonies at local war memorials in most cities, towns and villages. They are attended by civic dignitaries, ex-servicemen and women, members of local armed forces' regular and reserve units, the Combined Cadet Force (CCF) and youth organisations such as the Scouts, Guides, Boys' Brigade and Girls' Brigade. Wreaths of remembrance poppies are laid on the memorials and a two-minute silence is held at 11am.

Veterans For Peace UK walking to The Cenotaph under the banner 'Never Again'. Photo © Guy Smallman

In a letter to *The Guardian* in 2010, six veterans expressed their concern that the tone of remembrance events had changed. Ask your students what they think of the letter:

The Poppy Appeal is once again subverting Armistice Day. A day that should be about peace and remembrance is turned into a month-long drum roll of support for current wars. This year's campaign has been launched with showbiz hype. The true horror and futility of war is forgotten and ignored.

The public are being urged to wear a poppy in support of 'our Heroes'. There is nothing heroic about being blown up in a vehicle. There is nothing heroic about being shot in an ambush and there is nothing heroic about fighting in an unnecessary conflict.

Remembrance should be marked with the sentiment 'Never Again'.

www.guardian.co.uk/uk/2010/nov/05/poppies-and-heroes-remembrance-day

- Poppies: Ask your students if they wear a poppy around the time of Remembrance Sunday. Discuss the red poppy, the Peace Pledge Union's white poppy, the black poppy rose (for African/Black/West Indian/Pacific Island communities who contributed to the war effort), and the purple paw (for animal victims of war)

- Videos for discussion: a video about the white poppy can be found at https://youtu.be/0TVRTiCq27U. Also see https://youtu.be/NqTwe6iEfEo for the British Legion's 'Rethink Remembrance' campaign

16. www.gov.uk/government/policies/marking-relevant-national-events-and-ceremonies/supporting-pages/remembrance-sunday
17. For more information on the white poppy visit www.ppu.org.uk/learn/early/poppy3_early_years.html.

- Peace memorials: In Britain after World War I many of the memorials that were erected were called 'peace memorials'. Over time they all became universally known as 'war memorials'. To discover peace memorials go to www.ppu.org.uk/memorials/peace/london/index_peace_london1.html. Provide your students with a pack of colourful plasticine and a few other materials (such as foil, buttons, pipe cleaners, straws, etc.). In small groups ask them to build their own peace memorials.

Peacebuilding and the United Nations

World War I was a vast human tragedy and many people think it could have been avoided. After the war efforts were made to set up an organisation that would prevent war breaking out by creating an international forum where differences could be talked through and resolved. As a result, the League of Nations was created. It is considered a precursor to the United Nations (UN), which was created after World War II.

- UN fact-finding task: Explain to your students that there is a new British Prime Minister. She has decided that she wants to reassess Britain's membership of the UN. Ask your students to act as special advisers. In small groups they research and answer the following questions:

1. What's the purpose of the UN?

2. What's Britain's role in the UN?

Model United Nations General Assembly (MUNGA)

3. What good comes from the UN?

4. When has the UN failed?

5. What three suggestions would you have to make the UN more effective?

The special advisers then report back to the Prime Minister and provide an overall judgement as to whether they think Britain should remain a member. They should also include any other recommendations they have for the future of the UN. After listening to the presentation the Prime Minister (or her team) makes a decision.

There are lots of places to go to find out more about the UN. Here's one example:

- www.un.org/cyberschoolbus/humanrights/index.asp

To provide students with a more in-depth experience of the UN, organise a Model United Nations General Assembly (MUNGA). For more information go to www.una.org.uk/globe.

Additional resources

Resource A: Graffiti from Richmond Castle

> The only War which is worth fighting is the Class War. The Working Class of this Country have no quarrel with the Working Class of Germany or any other Country. Socialism stands for Internationalism. If the workers of all countries united & refused to fight, there would be no WAR
>
> the only war

Resource B: Loyalty ranking

My family	My friends
My school	My community
My church	My football team
My country	My…
My…	My…

Resource C: Big Grey and Little Red

We all know about the unfortunate experience of Little Red Riding Hood. There seems to be no doubt that the Wolf in the story behaved extremely badly. But why was that 'Big Grey' so hungry that he risked coming amongst humans? Our Big Grey could be a wolf… but could be human too!

Big Grey

You are Big Grey. Your ancestors have lived in the forest for many generations. The forest used to be much bigger and your ancestors used to roam freely and find plenty of food in the forest. There was a small village at the edge of the forest, but the settlers who lived there did not trouble your tribe and you had very little to do with them.

It is very different now. The village grew and grew into a large town and much of the forest has been cut down. The settlers have been hunting the Big Greys and there are not many of you left. There is also very little food left to find in what remains of the forest. So you are forced to look for food at the edges of the town and steal from the settlers. Life has become very dangerous.

Yesterday, you met this young settler called Little Red. She was carrying some delicious food in a basket, going along the path the settlers built through what was once part of the forest, but is now one of their 'parks'. You asked her for some food, but she refused rudely. You gathered that she was visiting her grandmother in the old part of the town. So you ran ahead, quickly shut the old woman in the cupboard and took her place in the bed, hurriedly putting on some of her clothes. When Little Red arrived, you tried to get the food from her, but she must have recognised you because she screamed, made an awful fuss so that an angry crowd of settlers armed with nasty weapons came after you and you were very lucky to escape – still starving.

Little Red

You live in a town which has been built near the edge of a forest. You live with your mother who has to work very hard to get enough money to feed you both and to pay for the other necessary things. Your grandmother lives in the old part of the town, which was originally just a small village. She is a very independent old lady and wants to live in the small cottage where she lived all her life. She is getting frail and cannot cook for herself every day, so you take her one meal a day, which your mother has prepared. The only way to her house (other than going a very long way round) takes you through the park which was once part of the forest. You have heard that Big Greys still live in the forest and sometimes wander into the park. You are rather frightened, but dare not tell your mother as she has enough troubles already.

Yesterday, as you were going to grandmother's house, suddenly this Big Grey came up to you and asked for food. Naturally you tried to get rid of him, but you must have said something about where you were going. When you got to grandmother's house, she was in bed and looked very strange. She asked you odd questions and was very eager to grab the food. As she reached towards you, you suddenly recognised Big Grey. Of course, you screamed for help and were very relieved when some builders and gardeners who worked next door rushed in with their tools and chased the Big Grey away.

You have been invited to talk to Big Grey in the presence of the new Mediation Service which tries to sort out problems in the town. You have heard that Big Greys are dying out as they do not have enough food in the forest. But you are mainly interested in knowing that you can safely deliver food for grandmother.

Mediator

You live in a town which has been built near the edge of a forest. The town has grown and the forest has shrunk. The Big Greys which live in the forest are also much reduced in number as they find less food and have been hunted by the town dwellers. They have recently become a nuisance and even a danger to the townsfolk as they come into the parks (which used to be part of the forest) and even to the streets near the edge of the town in search of food.

There is a conservation lobby[18] in the town which advocates measures to preserve the traditional life of the Big Greys. There is also a 'safe streets' lobby which wants strong measures to protect the townsfolk from the Big Greys.

Yesterday there was an incident when a Big Grey slunk up to a young girl named Little Red who was walking through the park to take food to her elderly grandmother who lives on her own. He asked for food, she was frightened and ran away. On entering her grandmother's house, she started talking to the figure in the bedroom whom she assumed to be her grandmother, only to find that it was Big Grey who (as it turned out) had shut the old lady in a cupboard and was now trying to trick Little Red into giving him the food. She shrieked for help and some neighbours, armed with garden tools, chased the Big Grey away. Both Big Grey and Little Red have agreed to come to the town Mediation Service.

These are brief notes for a mediator in this, or any other dispute:[19]

- You explain to both sides that your job is to help people in conflict to come to some agreement themselves, to decide on action which would improve the situation for both of them.

- Try to put them at their ease. Try to agree on ground rules (listening to each other, not interrupting, etc.).

- Try to structure the process, using the basic steps of mediation:

1. What has happened? What is the problem? Find a way of stating the problem so that both parties agree to the wording. This means that it may have to be a statement like: 'There is a disagreement about…'
2. Give each party a chance to say how he/she feels about the matter. Try to rephrase any accusations (e.g. 'you/he/she are/is…') as 'I' statements (e.g. 'I feel upset/angry because…'). Try to identify fears: '…so am I right that you are afraid that…?'.
3. Give each party a chance to say what would be her/his ideal solution and also what are her/his basic needs. Try to find out what is vital and what is less important to each side.
4. Encourage both sides to think of as many action steps as possible in this situation and to discuss the pros and cons of each option. Can they pick out any which suit them both and on which they can agree?

Throughout the process, try to build more trust. Thank each party for making any cooperative steps. Do not try to browbeat either side for the sake of forcing a solution. The conflict may be complex and may not be resolved at one stroke. It may be more realistic to aim for an agreement on some simple action steps than for a grand scheme which will solve everything.

From *Once upon a conflict: a fairytale manual of conflict resolution* by Tom Leimdorfer, Quaker Peace & Social Witness, 2014

18. A group of people that attempts to influence government on a particular issue.
19. A fuller description of the mediation process is given elsewhere in *Once upon a conflict*.

Further reading

Conscience: a World War I critical thinking project
A primary-level teachers' resource inspired by *Conviction*. Download for free at www.quaker.org.uk/education. To buy printed copies email the Quaker Centre at quakercentre@quaker.org.uk or call 020 7663 1030.

Voices of conscience
Six short films of personal experiences of war, conscientious objection and peacemaking. These moving films allow ordinary people to tell their personal stories, accompanied by photographs and illustrations from the period. Each film lasts for less than five minutes – accessible for all ages but ideal for Key Stages 2 and 3. They are accompanied by teachers' notes and are available in English or Welsh. To view the films go to www.vimeo.com/channels/voicesofconscience.
Web: www.breakingbarriers.org.uk.

Quaker service: a teachers' resource
This resource, for those aged 11–16, can also be used in primary or further education contexts. It uses the service provided by Quakers as an example through which to explore the wider issues of humanitarianism, refugee assistance, pacifism and peace. Its primary focus is on World War II, but World War I and the interwar period is briefly explored. For a copy email peaceedu@quaker.org.uk.

Once upon a conflict: A fairytale manual of of conflict resolution
by Tom Leimdorfer. Quaker Peace & Social Witness; first published 1992, new edition 2014. This book uses familiar stories to help readers explore the nature of conflict and find ways to handle it. It is inspired by the author's belief that, while we can't individually put an end to oppression and violent conflict, we can all be agents of change. Available from the Quaker Centre Bookshop, priced at £4. Visit www.quaker.org.uk/shop or phone 020 7663 1030 to order your copy.

Fly kites not drones
Fly Kites Not Drones is a creative non-violence project for young people. At its heart is the true story of Aymel, a boy who never really knew his father because of a drone strike. Teachers and anyone who works with young people can find resources here to learn about human rights and the effect of armed drones in the skies above us. Also available in Welsh. See www.flykitesnotdrones.org.

Teach Peace
In Teach Peace you will find a set of ten lesson plans for use as assemblies or workshops. The pack also contains follow-up activities and resources, prayers, and reflections on peace. See www.quaker.org.uk/resources/free-resources/teaching-resources-2.

The British Library – 'Pacifism and conscientious objectors' pack for young people aged 14 to 16
These activities can be downloaded at www.bl.uk/teaching-resources/civilians-pacifism-and-conscientious-objectors.

BBC Schools – World War One secondary school resources
These include an assembly pack exploring themes of remembrance, commemoration and peace. Visit www.bbc.co.uk/schools/0/ww1/25826265. **Peace Week**

The Peace Week pack
contains everything primary and secondary schools need to hold an off-timetable whole-school project week around peace and human rights. See www.quaker.org.uk/resources/free-resources/teaching-resources-2.

Places to find out more

Inspire: A project inviting young people to pledge action, and to collaborate with peers, as well as those in authority and their local communities, to create new peace initiatives www.oasisinspire.org.

The Imperial War Museums website: www.iwm.org.uk/collections/search

The Peace Pledge Union: www.ppu.org.uk. The oldest secular pacifist organisation in Britain has a range of eduction resources, as well as white poppy kits for remembrance: www.ppu.org.uk/learn.

The Northern Friends Peace Board: www.nfpb.org.uk/ww1

Movement for the Abolition of War: www.abolishwar.org.uk/resources.php

Coward: the reality of life on the front lines in World War One
A 28-minute drama that brings to light the brutal treatment soldiers received for suffering what would now be known as shell shock. Available on youtube at https://youtu.be/nOcEX3dYn3s.

Arming All Sides: the arms trade and the First World War
Explore the links between the arms trade and war at http://armingallsides.on-the-record.org.uk.

For more on peace education
The Peace Education Network: www.peace-education.org.uk/education-for-peace

Peace One Day: www.peaceoneday.org.

The Peaceful Schools Movement: www.peacefulschools.org.uk.

The Peer Mediation Network: www.peermediationnetwork.org.uk.

Two Friends' Ambulance Unit (FAU) members transporting bread. Date unknown.

About Quakers

Quakers share a way of life, not a set of beliefs. Their unity is based on shared understanding and a shared practice of silent worship, where they seek a communal stillness.

Quakers seek to experience God directly, within themselves and in their relationships with others and the world around them. They meet together for worship in local meetings, which are open to all who wish to attend.

Quakers try to live with honesty and integrity. This means speaking truth to all, including people in positions of power. The Quaker commitment to peace arises from the conviction that love is at the heart of existence and that all human beings are unique and equal.

This leads Quakers to put their faith into action by working locally and globally to change the systems that cause injustice and violent conflict.

Britain Yearly Meeting of the Religious Society of Friends (Quakers)
Registered charity number 1127633

Friends House, 173 Euston Road, London, NW1 2BJ

Follow us on social media @BritishQuakers.
www.quaker.org.uk